CHOMSKY

A BEGINNER'S GUIDE

Virginia S Peckham
601 W. Main Rd
Little Compton R.I. 02837

CHOMSKY

A BEGINNER'S GUIDE

MICHAEL DEAN

Hodder & Stoughton

A MEMBER OF THE HODDER HEADLINE GROUP

Orders: please contact Bookpoint Ltd, 130 Milton Park, Abingdon, Oxon OX14 4SB.
Telephone: (44) 01235 827720, Fax: (44) 01235 400454. Lines are open from 9.00–6.00,
Monday to Saturday, with a 24-hour message answering service.
You can also order through our website www.madaboutbooks.co.uk

British Library Cataloguing in Publication Data
A catalogue record for this title is available from The British Library

ISBN 0 340 84500 7

First published 2003
Impression number   10 9 8 7 6 5 4 3 2 1
Year 2007 2006 2005 2004 2003

Copyright © 2003 Michael Dean

Typeset by Transet Limited, Coventry, England.
Printed in Great Britain for Hodder & Stoughton Educational, a division of Hodder Headline
Plc, 338 Euston Road, London NW1 3BH by Cox & Wyman, Reading, Berks.

CONTENTS

Introduction

Noam Chomsky is the world's most visited person on the Internet and the most quoted man alive today. *The Arts and Humanities Citation Index* for 1980–92 lists him as the eighth most quoted person of all time, just behind Freud.

In fact, it could be argued that Chomsky's work on the way children acquire language is so fundamental that its significance can be compared to Darwin's account of evolution and Freud's theory of the unconscious.

The comparison with Charles Darwin, in terms of the influence the two men had on the world, is interesting. In 1859 Charles Darwin wrote *On the Origin of Species*, a book that changed how we see ourselves as human beings. It said that all life came from earlier life: evolution. Chomsky's ideas on the human mind started a debate that also changed our view of the sort of beings we are.

And just as Darwin's ideas prompted the famous Oxford Debate of 1869, so Chomsky's ideas about the human mind started a debate, carried out in print, with B.F. Skinner, a psychology professor at Harvard. This is described in more detail in Chapter 2, but here is a summary:

Skinner believed that we learn a language by hearing, for example, the word 'chair', seeing a chair and then saying the word 'chair.' When we get it right, our 'reward' is that people understand us. This is a mechanistic view of language and the mind. It sees people as machines.

Chomsky, however, saw language as something that 'grows in the mind' (*Language and Thought*, 1994, p. 29). It's like growing an apple from seed. Yes, it needs the right conditions to grow, but we are born with the seed as part of our minds. That is how we acquire language. And we use it creatively. Children and adults can say sentences that they cannot possibly have heard before. This is species specific; only humans can do it.

Having and using language, Chomsky thinks, is part of what makes human beings creative individuals. Chomsky even speaks of 'I–language', which is his term for one person's individual language in that person's mind and how it is used.

So Chomsky's victory in argument over Skinner saw the triumph of the view of human beings as thinking, creative individuals over the view of them as machines that react automatically to what happens to them.

Chomsky's insights into language led him back to philosophers like Descartes (1596–1650), who had also seen the ability to think as central to what makes a person a human being. They then led him forward to detailed theories of how language works in shaping the thoughts of every individual.

But Chomsky is famous for his political views as well as for his work on language. He has opposed American foreign policy from the war in Vietnam in the 1960s to the US role in events in Kosovo and East Timor at the turn of this century. And his views on the attack on New York on 11 September 2001 are typically forthright and controversial.

James Sobran, an American columnist, called Chomsky 'a man without a sect.' He has never belonged to or identified himself with any group at all. He is a renegade; a great individualist. Politically he is an anarchist (see Chapter 6). It will be argued in this book that the view of life that made Chomsky see language as individual thought is the same view of life that made him reject all groups in favour of the individual. If people are seen as complex, creative beings it is easier to care about what happens to them than if they are seen as machines. The death and suffering of individuals has concerned Chomsky greatly. If he thinks a group is responsible for something that is wrong, it is irrelevant to him that it is a group to which he may belong – for example, the United States because he is an American, or Israel because he is Jewish. He will still condemn that group. He is always on the side of the individual.

Chomsky has rejected group membership as completely as he has rejected the view of a person as a kind of machine. He views each and every human as a complex entity whose expression of individuality through language is interesting and whose life matters.

Linguistics and Politics in Early Life

THE CHILD IS FATHER TO THE MAN

Wordsworth's saying that the child is father to the man was never truer than when applied to Avram Noam Chomsky. Both the linguist and the political commentator are there in embryo in his childhood.

Chomsky was born on 7 December 1928, the oldest son of Dr William Chomsky and Elsie Simonsky, in Philadelphia, Pennsylvania, USA. Chomsky's own account of his parents is characteristically modest. In an interview with David Barsamian, he described them as 'Hebrew school teachers, so sort of lower middle class.' In fact Dr William Chomsky started teaching at the religious school of the Mikveh Israel congregation, but eventually became its principal, while continuing to research in medieval Hebrew language in his free time. The *New York Times* called him 'one of the world's greatest Hebrew grammarians' in its obituary in 1977.

William Chomsky worked on a study of a thirteenth-century Hebrew grammar called *David Kimhi's Hebrew Grammar (Mikhlol)*. Noam Chomsky read this scholarly work while his father was still working on it. He was 12 at the time.

He also read the Talmud at home, in Hebrew. The Talmud is both the Jewish law (called the Mishnah) and a commentary on the law (the Gemara). 'My idea of the ideal text is still the Talmud' says Chomsky (quoted in Barsky, *Noam Chomsky: A Life of Dissent*, 1948, p.10), 'I love the idea of parallel texts, ... texts commenting on texts.' It is possible that this parellelism gave Chomsky the idea that a text can do two things at once; it can operate on more than one level. Perhaps this was the inspiration for his later research into the 'deep structure' that lies beneath all texts (see Chapter 5).

he influence of Chomsky's mother, Elsie, was more on the political side. She was more left wing than her husband. 'Remember I grew up in the Depression,' Chomsky reminds us (Ben Isitt, *Noam Chomsky Interview*, March 2000, p.7). 'My earliest childhood memories are miserable old people coming to the house ... and trying to sell rags or apples just to survive ...' **The Depression** was a time of great poverty and unemployment, which began in 1929 and continued throughout most of the 1930s. But it

KEYWORD

The Depression: The Depression began in October 1929 with the Wall Street Crash, the collapse of the American Stock Market. It lasted throughout most of the 1930s and was really only ended by the Second World War (1939–45).

was also a time of great political awareness and political debate.

> Jewish working class culture in New York was very unusual. It was highly intellectual, very poor; a lot of people had no jobs at all and others lived in slums and so on. But it was a rich and lively intellectual culture: Freud, Marx ... and so forth. That was, I think the most intellectual culture during my early teens.
>
> (Chomsky interview with James Peck in *The Chomsky Reader*, 1988, p.11)

As well as his mother, another family influence on Chomsky's early left-wing politics was his uncle. The young Noam used to go from Philadelphia to New York by train and there, at the corner of 72nd Street and Broadway, his uncle had a newspaper kiosk. That was the place he claimed to have gained his political education. After listening to the poor intellectuals at the kiosk, young Noam would wander around the Fourth Avenue second-hand bookshops or visit the office of the anarchist magazine, *Frei Arbeiter Stimme*. This influenced his later anarchist political views. The magazine published the German anarchist Rudolf Rocker whose works Chomsky started to read (see Chapter 6).

EARLY INFLUENCES IN LINGUISTICS AND POLITICS

Even in his early years we see the individualism that underlay Chomsky's work in **linguistics** and politics. Talking of this time in his early youth, Chomsky says 'I didn't have any affiliation to any group ... Partly it was that I'm not much of a "joiner" I guess.' (interview with James Peck in *The Chomsky Reader*, 1988, p.10), and that 'he always felt out of tune with almost everything around him.'

Chomsky was brought up in an orthodox Jewish household. Robert F. Barsky, Chomsky's biographer, who knows him personally, writes:

> From a very early age Noam and David [Chomsky's brother, who was five years younger] were immersed in the scholarship, culture and traditions of Judaism and the Hebrew language ...
>
> (*Noam Chomsky a Life of Dissent*, 1948, p.12)

Zionism, the idea of Jewish people returning to Israel, was one of the hot political topics debated at the Chomsky family's dinner table and at his uncle's newspaper kiosk.

Chomsky got to know his future wife and life-long partner, Carol Schatz, at Hebrew School (though they 'met' when he was five and she was three). And if he needed a reminder that he was Jewish, it was provided by the fact that he belonged to the only Jewish family in a Irish and German Catholic neighbourhood. There he encountered bitter anti-semitism and open support for the Nazis until December 1941. But Noam was to oppose prejudice from whichever side it came. When a camp for German prisoners of war was set up right next to his school, some of the kids started taunting the prisoners, but Chomsky defended the Germans and tried to get them to stop, even though, as

KEYWORD

Linguistics: Linguistics is the scientific study of language. Sometimes it studies the sounds, words and grammar of one language. As a result of Chomsky's work, it can also study the relationship between particular languages and the universal characteristics that form the basis of all languages. It can also look at the sociological or psychological aspects of communication.

he recalls, he was a much more committed anti-Nazi than the kids who were baiting the prisoners.

At this time a global event was to influence Chomsky's politics greatly: the dropping of the atomic bomb on Hiroshima. Chomsky recalls that he literally couldn't talk to anybody and that he felt completely isolated. It was by no means the last time that he was to feel that way.

THE INFLUENCE OF HIS SCHOOLS

From the age of just two years old until he was 12, Chomsky went to the Oak Lane Country Day School which was run on **Deweyite** principles, that is the principles of the philosopher **John Dewey**. In 'Democracy and Education', a lecture given by Chomsky at Loyola University Chicago, 19 October 1994, he acknowledges Dewey's influence '... his thought was a strong influence on me in my formative years – in fact from about age two on' and he described Dewey as 'one of the outstanding thinkers of the past century.'

At Oak Lane children from different backgrounds and with different levels of ability were encouraged to develop their individual interest freed from the competitive need to be a good student. The goal was self-development, not good marks or coming top of the class. In the 1994 Chicago lecture Chomsky quotes another influence on him, **Bertrand Russell**, 'one of the very few people I actually admire,' to explain the views on education that were formed at Oak Lane: shifting over from Dewey to Bertrand Russell, he describes the purpose of

KEYWORDS

Deweyite (John Dewey 1859–1952): John Dewey was a philosopher, a psychologist, an educator and a social critic. He was a pioneer of the progressive school movement. His interest in education, set out in *Democracy and Education* (1916) led him to be a fierce social critic. In his lecture in Chicago in 1994 Chomsky quoted a sentence of Dewey's that sums up his educational and social philosophy: 'The ultimate aim of production is not production of goods, but the production of free human beings associated with one another on terms of equality.'

Bertrand Russell (1872–1970): Bertrand Russell was a socialist, a pacifist and a distinguished philosopher and mathematician. He also ran a progressive school called Beacon Hill from 1928–32. His picture is on the wall of Chomsky's office at Massachusetts Institute of Technology.

education as 'to give a sense of the value of things other than domination.'

In the Oak Lane school magazine *The Odyssey*, Noam Chomsky, aged ten, wrote an article on the fall of Barcelona in the Spanish Civil War (1936–9). Barcelona had fallen to the fascist forces of the right in January 1939 and Chomsky recalls how affected he was by that event.

At the age of 12, Chomsky moved from Oak Lane to Central High School, also in Philadelphia. Despite discovering that he was intelligent and getting good marks, he yearned for the freedom of Oak Lane, and his lasting view of the purpose of education (which was that it should allow the growing principle of life to take its own course) had been formed by Oak.

But from this point on, Chomsky would follow his mentor Dewey in two things: one was in his educational ideas and the other was in not making any distinction between education and work. In other words, the goal of all activity, at school or at the workplace, was to provide creative tasks to develop the individual, not to produce things within a system. These ideas were developed later into libertarianism and anarchism (see Chapter 6), but the seeds were sown at the age of 12.

CHOMSKY'S ACADEMIC RISE

In 1945 Chomsky started at the University of Pennsylvania (often abbreviated to Penn) at the remarkably young age of 16. He was generally unhappy at Penn, finding the institutional structure as stifling as he had found it at Central High School. But once again the linguistics and the politics were to come together, as they had in his home life as a child.

Chomsky was living at home and teaching Hebrew to pay for his studies at university. He was also the only undergraduate in the university studying Arabic, partly 'because of his interest in Semitic linguistics, which stemmed from his father's work in that area, and partly through the influence of Georgio Levi Della Vida' (as described in an interview with James Peck in *The Chomsky Reader*, 1988, p.7). Della Vida had had to leave Italy because of the rise of fascism in that country. A leading left-wing figure, he was an important political influence on Chomsky.

Chomsky himself always downplays any link between the linguistic and the political sides of his work and thought, but Della Vida's influence on Chomsky as a young man is one of many examples throughout his life where the two have come together and intertwined.

Just as Chomsky was intending to leave university and pursue his political interests, he met a man who was to influence his life greatly. It was 1947, Chomsky had just turned 18, and the man taught modern linguistics at the University of Pennsylvania. His name was Zellig Harris. Barsky (1948, p.50) argues that 'it was not Harris's linguistics that first attracted Chomsky: he was tantalized by his Professor's politics.'

Harris, Chomsky recalls, was an extraordinary person who greatly influenced many young people in those days. Under Harris's influence, Chomsky began to study philosophy and mathematics at Penn. The philosophy later underpinned his linguistic work, because it took him back to Descartes and a view of language and mind which he has held ever since (see Chapter 2). He has also frequently used mathematics as a tool in linguistic research.

And, of course, Harris's own courses were in linguistics. The first reading Chomsky ever did in linguistics was the proofs of Harris's book *Methods in Structural Linguistics*. But crucially for Chomsky's enjoyment of study, he was freed from the oppressive institutional structure of the university. This was because the unorthodox Harris held most of his classes in the Horn and Hardart restaurant, or in his own flat. There a small number of students sharing political and other interests, apart from linguistics, met all day and discussed a wide variety of topics. Chomsky had almost no contact with the university outside these unorthodox sessions and he obtained what he describes as highly unconventional B.A. and M.A. degrees.

Most commentators see Chomsky's work in linguistics, which is outlined in Chapters 4 and 5, as a break with Harris's, although some (notably the leading British linguist, John Lyons and Katz and Bevor in America) see Chomsky's work as in some ways a development of what Harris was doing. Either way, there is little doubt that Harris shaped Chomsky's later life.

Harris advised Chomsky to take philosophy courses with Nelson Goodman at Penn. Chomsky's knowledge of philosophy was later to revolutionize first his own and then the world's approach to linguistics, a story outlined in Chapter 2.

Goodman recommended Chomsky for the Society of Fellows at Harvard and he was admitted in 1951. Being in the Society of Fellows carried a stipend and so for the first time Chomsky could study without having to earn money. His doctorate which (technically) came from Penn even though Chomsky had not been there since 1951, was obtained in 1955. It was a chapter of the unconventional book Chomsky was working on at the time called *Logical Structure of Linguistic Theory*.

At the age of 29, Chomsky became an Associate Professor at Massachusetts Institute of Technology. MIT (as it is known) is now the hub of linguistics study world-wide, mainly because Chomsky is there, but before he arrived it had no record in linguistics studies at all. Chomsky became a full Professor there at the age of 32. This may look like an orthodox career progression, but it certainly is not. By this time Chomsky's work in linguistics was so different to every other linguist's work that it was, as Chomsky later put it, simply not recognized as related to linguistics at all.

In later chapters we look in more detail at what this work actually was, but for now let's leave the last word to Chomsky, in his own wry style:

> The reason I'm teaching at MIT is ... I had no prospects in a university that had a tradition in any field related to linguistics ... because the work I was doing simply was not recognized as related to that field. ... And, therefore, I ended up in an electronics laboratory. I don't know how to handle anything more complex than a tape recorder, and not even that, but I've been in an electronics laboratory for the last thirty years.

(quoted in *The Chomsky Reader*, 1988, p.15)

✻ ✻ ✻ SUMMARY ✻ ✻ ✻

● Chomsky's father influenced his early study of texts and it is possible that studying the Talmud, in particular, gave him the idea that language can operate on more than one level, which he used in his early linguistic theories.

● Chomsky's mother and uncle were early influences on his politics but the biggest influence was being brought up in the Depression of the 1930s.

● Chomsky's political views were partly formed by seeing German POWs taunted and then defending them, but especially by the USA dropping an atomic bomb on Hiroshima. Both events affected him because he identified with the victims as individuals.

● Chomsky's first school led to his love of creative freedom and loathing of institutional constraint. It was a Deweyite school and John Dewey was a strong influence, as was Bertrand Russell.

● The strongest personal influence on Chomsky's early life was Zellig Harris, who set him on the road to study and started his reading in linguistics. Chomsky's linguistic ideas arose out of Harris's – mainly as a reaction against them, although some linguists see Chomsky's ideas as a development of Harris's.

Language and Mind 2

RATIONALISM VERSUS EMPIRICISM

The mind is studied in different ways in linguistics, psychology and philosophy and Chomsky does not see these disciplines as separate from each other. The starting point for his view of language comes from philosophy.

In philosophy, there is a basic distinction between empiricist and rationalist philosophers. Empiricists believe that all knowledge comes from experience – and by experience they mean sense data: what we see, hear, smell, feel and so on. This sense data comes from the world around us, so empiricism sees the environment as important. Rationalists, on the other hand, believe that the mind – reason – is the primary source of human knowledge, and the means by which we interpret sense data.

Chomsky is a rationalist – a believer in the primacy of mind – and is strongly influenced by the French philosopher **Descartes**. Descartes is known to many people for his Latin motto *Cogito ergo sum* (I think, therefore I am), demonstrating the importance to him of mind and cognitive (from Latin *cogito* – to think) philosophy.

KEYWORD

René Descartes (1596–1650): Like Plato and St Augustine before him, Descartes believed that we can reach knowledge only through reason. He tried to unify thought into one coherent system (i.e. one system that makes sense). Descartes also wrote a *Discourse on Method*. Methodology is about how new knowledge should be discovered. Descartes believed that philosophy should start with the simple and move to the complex. It should break down a compound problem into as many single factors as possible. Then the simplest idea of all is studied.

All these ideas – unifying thought, the importance of mind and the methodology of proceeding from the simple to the complex – influenced Chomsky greatly.

THE CREATIVE USE OF LANGUAGE

Followers of Descartes are known as Cartesians. Chomsky describes himself as a believer in 'Cartesian common sense' (speaking to Bill Moyers in *A World of Ideas*, PBS public TV, USA, 1988). He drew on the work not only of Descartes but of other Cartesian philosophers like Cordemoy and La Forge. In works like La Forge's *Traité de l'esprit de l'homme* (*A Treatise on the Spirit of Man*) the Cartesians developed the idea that human thought and human language is so complex that it cannot be explained in terms of the body alone, or as a reaction to sense data.

Only a second substance (as the Cartesians called it), namely the mind, could account for the complexity of thought and language. The Cartesians were fascinated by what this second substance, the mind, actually was, but Chomsky is not. '... the whole issue of whether there's a physical basis for mental structures is a rather empty issue' (Radio discussion with Stuart Hampshire, *The Listener*, 30 May 1968). Unlike the Cartesians, Chomsky is interested in what the mind *does*, with regard to language, not what it *is* or how it works.

And what interests Chomsky, within all the things the mind does, is 'the creative aspect of language use,' the distinctively human ability to express new thoughts and to understand entirely new expressions of thought (see Chomsky, *Language and Mind*, 1972, p.6). The normal use of language is innovative, says Chomsky. ' ... much of what we say in the course of normal language use is entirely new, not a repetition of anything we have heard before' (ibid, p.12).

The fact that human beings use their creative minds to make entirely new sentences every day of their lives is basic to Chomsky's view of language, the mind and humankind. If all human beings, whichever language they speak, can use language creatively in the same way, then there must be linguistic universals underlying all languages, which are fundamentally the same. Chomsky called these linguistic universals *Universal Grammar* (see keyword box, p.12).

Can the existence of Universal Grammar be proved? Not really. But Chomsky was proved right about humans' creative use of language in innovative sentences by a fascinating experiment by Richard Ohlmann at Wesleyan University.

Ohlmann showed 25 people a cartoon and asked them to describe it in one sentence. All the descriptions were different. Then he put all the words used in the descriptions into a computer program, which generated all the possible grammatically correct combinations, using those words. There were 19.8 billion different combinations.

It would take ten trillion years – 20,000 times the estimated age of the earth – to say all the possible sentences in English that use exactly 20 words. That gives some idea of how long we would have to listen, if we waited to hear a sentence before being able to say it.

IS THE CREATIVE USE OF LANGUAGE SPECIES SPECIFIC?

Chomsky has devoted a lot of his life to working out just how we manage to come out with entirely new sentences that we have not heard before. But he follows Descartes in believing that having such a complex, creative mind is what distinguishes a human from an automaton (a robot) or an animal. In other words the creative use of language is 'species specific' and that 'the acquisition of even the barest rudiments of language is quite beyond the capacities of an otherwise intelligent ape' (*Language and Mind,* 1972, p.59).

This is debatable. A chimpanzee called Washoe was taught ASL (American Sign Language) using pictures. Washoe learned over a hundred signs and came up with combinations of them that she had not been taught – creative use of language. Another ape called Sarah was taught to communicate using coloured plastic tokens. She mastered complexities like conditional sentences (using 'if') and concepts like the difference between 'some apples' and 'no apples' which involve an understanding of the structure of the sentence. A good introduction to the views of those who think that animal language is both more developed and closer to a human's, is *Apes, Men and Language* by Eugene Linden (Penguin Books, 1976).

People who disagree with Chomsky about creative use of language being species specific often use the word 'language' in a different sense to Chomsky. There is no doubt that *some* language (the rudiments) can be learned by hearing or seeing and then repeating, but Chomsky would regard this limited ability as very much a side-issue.

CHOMSKY'S STARTING POINT OF LINGUISTIC ANALYSIS

Chomsky not only followed the Cartesians in his theory of mind, but also took their practical work in linguistic analysis as his starting point. Cartesian scholars were working on a language **grammar** at Port Royal, France, in 1660.

In the Port Royal grammar, the starting point, the compound problem which has to be broken down and made simple, was *the phrase*. Chomsky himself gives this example of a phrase 'Invisible God created the visible world.' (*Language and Mind*, 1974, p.16). This phrase can be broken down, going from complex to simple, like this: The subject of the phrase is 'invisible God' and the predicate (the rest of the sentence that is not the subject) is 'created the visible world.' That predicate is still a complex idea that can be simplified further into 'the visible world' and the verb 'created'.

> ## KEYWORD
>
> **Grammar:** The word grammar is used in many different ways. Descriptive grammar 'describes the grammatical constructions which are used in a language' (Crystal, *Cambridge Encyclopaedia of Linguis-tics* p. 88) i.e. used in ONE language. Chomsky, following the Cartesians, became interested in theoretical grammar which 'goes beyond the study of individual languages (to) ... linguistic universals (which) can be applied in the investigation of human language.' i.e. all human languages, not just one. Chomsky calls these linguistic universals Universal Grammar.

All that is surface structure, but as early as 1660, the Port Royal grammarians also discovered the deep structure of texts, which Chomsky too had found as a child, reading the Talmud. The deep structure consists of propositions – ideas. There are three propositions in the phrase above: first, that God is invisible: secondly that he created the world and thirdly that the world is visible. That is the deep structure of the phrase.

ORTHODOX LINGUISTIC ANALYSIS BEFORE CHOMSKY

What was going on in the early days of linguistics studies was very different to Chomsky's interest in theoretical grammar and his search for the Universal Grammar that underlies all language and explains its creativity. The founding fathers of the study of linguistics were empiricists. Linguistics started in the USA as a branch of anthropology. Early leaders in the new field were anthropologists like Franz Boas (1852–1942) and Edward Sapir (1884–1939), Professor of Anthropology at Yale. Boas, Sapir and their followers set out to produce descriptive grammars of Native American languages. They identified the elements of surface structure only, not deep structure.

Their methodology (the way they worked) was different from the Cartesians and from Chomsky, too. The early linguists used *discovery procedures*, which they applied to *attested language* – nearly always written. In other words, they found a piece of writing and tried to work out how the language of that particular piece of writing worked. To Chomsky this was limiting. With his usual refreshing readiness to speculate, he believed a linguist could proceed by 'intuition, guesswork, all sorts of partial methodological hints, reliance on past experience etc' (*Syntactic Structures*, 1957, p.56).

Even more important than the methodology, the underlying issue was what exactly should be investigated. Chomsky was interested not so much in what people could be proved to have said (attested language) but what they could have said, what they had the capacity to say. One way of expressing this difference was the Swiss linguist Ferdinand de Saussure's distinction between *langue* and *parole*. *Langue* was the corpus of a language, all the words or sentences in English, for example. *Parole* was the knowledge of English possessed by a speaker of it. This later became known as the speaker's *competence* in the language, and it was that which Chomsky wanted to account for and explain.

Influence in linguistics passed from Boas and Sapir to Leonard Bloomfield (1887–1949), one of the founding fathers of the Linguistic Society of America (1924). Bloomfield's structuralism ignored meaning and looked at how words fit together one after the other (syntax) and how the system of sound works (phonology).

It led to *finite state grammars*, which explained a sentence as a string of words going from left to right and tried to account for the next word in terms of what had gone before. So if the first two words are 'She goes …' the next word might be 'to'. This ignores any of the mental processes which the Cartesians and Chomsky were interested in. It attempts to explain one piece of language, rather than language itself.

TWO VIEWS OF WHAT HUMAN BEINGS ARE

Bloomfield and his followers thought that an organism (all organisms, including people) was best understood in terms of *responses to stimuli*. These stimuli come from the prime influence in the empiricist school of thought – the environment. And the leading supporter of the stimulus-response theory was **B. F. Skinner**.

In 1957, the same year as Chomsky wrote the ground breaking account of his own linguistic

KEYWORD

Burrhus Frederic Skinner (1904–1990) and behaviourism: After a false start as a writer, B. F. Skinner studied psychology in Minneapolis, Minnesota. He became known to the wider world during World War II, when pigeons were needed to carry messages. Skinner developed a way of training them. He put them in a box known as a 'Skinner Box' and devised a system of rewards and punishments to get them to do what he wanted. The system was called 'operant conditioning.'

Operant conditioning: A way of totally controlling behaviour – i.e. behaviourism. Skinner applied it to his children too, putting them in a playpen like Skinner's Box and controlling their behaviour by rewards and punishments. The assumption was that pigeons and people are malleable (a behaviourist word) and you can do what you like with them, given the right conditioning. Skinner went on to develop variants on the theme of conditioning: 'shaping behaviour,' 'behaviour modification,' 'negative reinforcement' and so on.

system, *Syntactic Structures*, B. F. Skinner published *Verbal Behaviour*. Chomsky reviewed *Verbal Behaviour* in 1959 in the academic journal *Language* (Volume 35, Number 1, pp.26–58). It is difficult to overstate the importance of this review. It signalled the beginning of the end for behaviourism; it made us see ourselves as thinking, creative beings, not as animals or robots capable of being influenced to do anything.

Stephen Pinker, Professor of Psychology at MIT and author of several popular books on linguistics including *The Language Instinct* (Penguin Books, 1994) put it like this:

> Chomsky gave the first, fatal shot to the school of behaviourism and made theories of innate mental structure respectable after centuries of their being unthinkable.
>
> (*The Guardian*, 20 January 2001)

The importance of Chomsky's victory – and it was a total victory – goes far beyond linguistics. It is one of the times that the conjunction between Chomsky's political and linguistic opinions is most obvious, despite Chomsky's own denial that the two have anything to do with each other. Here is Pinker again: '... if people are ignorant, malleable creatures who can be modified by experience and training, they can be controlled for their own good.'

Chomsky's polemical, ironic style has its critics. (Pinker, who is basically a supporter of Chomsky but who never loses his objectivity, is one of them.) But the controlled passion of Chomsky's prose was never put to better use than here. Here is one phrase, just to give you the flavour. Chomsky described Skinner's behaviourist world as 'like a well-run concentration camp.'

This battle over how we see ourselves, our view of what a human being is, was fought on the battleground of linguistics between two American professors who, with an irony Chomsky perhaps appreciated, were also neighbours. Skinner moved to Cambridge, Massachusetts in 1948, when he became a professor at Harvard. MIT, where Chomsky is a

Professor, is also in Cambridge Massachusetts and Chomsky had been there since 1957.

Skinner's fundamental position was that complex human behaviour like speech can be explained by the same variables such as *stimulus*, *reinforcement* (i.e. reward) and *deprivation* that can influence the behaviour of pigeons. Skinner denies or ignores what is happening in the speaker's head – the entire rationalist, or 'mentalist' field of study.

The difficulty this presents the rationalist opponent of Skinner (or at least, a lesser opponent than Chomsky) is that nobody really understood the process by which the mind produced speech. By simply observing speech as behaviour Skinner was – as Chomsky acknowledged – limiting a complex problem to something simple enough to study. The methodology, though not the conclusions, was defensible.

As there was not enough known about the mentalist position to defend it as a credible alternative, Chomsky demolished Skinner on his own ground. Skinner's variables, Chomsky argued, could only be applied to complex human behaviour in the most gross and superficial way. Chomsky then proceeded to dismantle Skinner's system piece by piece. Here is just one example. This is Chomsky arguing with typical irony that according to Skinner's system the only response to the stimulus of a Dutch picture is the word 'Dutch':

> A typical example of stimulus control for Skinner would be the response to ... a painting with the response 'Dutch'. According to Skinner this response is asserted to be 'under the control of extremely subtle properties' of the physical object or event. Suppose instead of saying 'Dutch' we had said 'Clashes with the wallpaper', 'I thought you liked abstract work', 'Never saw it before', 'Tilted', 'Hanging too low', 'Beautiful', 'Hideous', 'Remember our camping trip last summer?' or whatever else might come into our minds when looking at a picture.
>
> (*Language*, Volume 35, Number 1, 1959)

Chomsky asserts the glorious diversity and creativity of the individual here, and destroys the argument of those who wish to bring it low.

❋ ❋ ❋ *SUMMARY* ❋ ❋ ❋

• Chomsky's **rationalist** (or mentalist) view of language was influenced by Descartes. He believes that some sort of mental process enables people to create language that they have never heard before.

• Chomsky therefore disagrees with empiricist approaches which emphasize the primacy of sense data and the role of the environment.

• Chomsky has followed the early mentalist grammars of language in his belief in a **deep structure** of propositions (ideas) underlying the **surface structure** of language.

• Chomsky sees language as **species specific**. In other words, that it is unique to humans and that animals do not use language in any meaningful sense.

• Chomsky is interested in the study of **theoretical grammar** to find **language universals** which underlie all languages. He called these universals **Universal Grammar**.

• To do this he studied **perfect** or **idealized** language (though spoken, not written). He examined what de Saussure called **parole** rather than **langue** and what others have called **competence** rather than **performance**. In other words he was not interested in real examples of **attested language**, but in example sentences of the spoken language which illustrated how the underlying system works.

• When studying language, Chomsky follows Descartes in proceeding from the simple to the complex, using intuition where necessary. He rejects the 'discovery procedures' of earlier linguists.

• Chomsky has succeeded in making his stance the new orthodoxy ('The one to beat,' as Pinker puts it). He single-handedly demolished the behaviourist school, represented by B. F. Skinner, which sees language as a part of **stimulus-response** learned behaviour.

3 Child Language Acquisition

The study of child language acquisition – how children learn language – did not start with Chomsky, but his revolution in linguistics provided the impetus for the study of children and language. This revolution, as we saw in Chapter 2, was Chomsky's establishment of a 'mentalist' orthodoxy, that the mind plays a creative role, paving the way for the study of what is going on in the mind.

The empiricist position, opposing this, became a minority view. Empiricists, deriving their philosophical inspiration from John Locke (1632–1704) and led at the moment by the linguist John Searle (born 1932), argue against any form of unconscious rules operating in the mind. They say that the incoming sense-data, speech, is heard by the child, organized into patterns, and then repeated. They see language acquisition in terms of learning and teaching.

Chomsky's mentalist view is very different from this. In Section V of his review of Skinner's *Verbal Behaviour* in 1959, Chomsky produced a view of child language acquisition which he kept well into later life. The view was that children absorb language unconsciously, provided that they hear it around them. They do not learn it. They are not taught it by parents or by any other person or means:

> It is simply not true that children can learn language only through 'meticulous care' on the part of adults who shape their verbal repertoire ... Even a very young child who has not yet acquired a minimal repertoire from which to form new utterances may imitate a word quite well on an early try, with no attempt on the part of his parents to teach it to him.
>
> (Chomsky: Language Section V)

THE LANGUAGE ACQUISITION DEVICE (LAD) AND THE CRITICAL PERIOD

Children are not born with empty minds, which parents fill with language that the child then imitates. On the contrary, children are genetically disposed to structure language. They are born with relevant information that aids language acquisition. The language they apply this information to, of course, is the language they hear. So a child who hears Chinese will grow up speaking Chinese, but the rule-mechanism the child is applying to speak Chinese is the same one as an English or American child is using to speaking English. Except that Chomsky did not call it a rule mechanism. He called it a **Language Acquisition Device** (LAD), later using the term *language faculty* for the same thing.

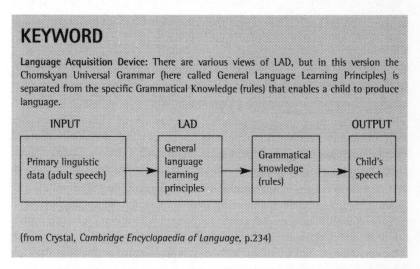

KEYWORD

Language Acquisition Device: There are various views of LAD, but in this version the Chomskyan Universal Grammar (here called General Language Learning Principles) is separated from the specific Grammatical Knowledge (rules) that enables a child to produce language.

INPUT   LAD   OUTPUT

Primary linguistic data (adult speech) → General language learning principles → Grammatical knowledge (rules) → Child's speech

(from Crystal, *Cambridge Encyclopaedia of Language*, p.234)

The many languages of the world are often thought to be very different from each other, but the LAD theory accounts for something more surprising – that there are great similarities across languages.

The capacity for organizing words into relationships of words to each other is inherent, it is in our minds. That is why languages, all languages, contain such striking similarities. As Chomsky memorably put it 'apart from differences in the lexicon (the words) there is only one human language.'

Here is an example of how similar languages are. It demonstrates that various languages form relative clauses in the same way. A 'clause' is a group of words, smaller than a sentence, that contains a subject and a predicate. So 'I read the book that you read.' contains two clauses: 'I read the book' and 'that you read.' The second clause, 'that you read' is a relative clause. Relative clauses use relative pronouns like 'that', 'which', 'who', 'whose' and so on, to relate one clause to another. Relative clauses basically give extra information about the main clause. 'That I read' gives extra information about 'the book'.

Here are examples from English and French, in each case the relative clause is in bold.

> The man **that I saw** was your brother.
> I read the book **that you read**.

> L'homme **que j'ai vu** était ton frère.
> J'ai lu le livre **que tu as lu**.
>
> (from N. Smith and D. Wilson, *Modern Linguistics – the Results of Chomsky's Revolution*, 1990)

Hebrew uses the same system but with an extra pronoun (a word that replaces a noun – like 'he' or 'him' can replace a noun like 'John'). The asterisk in these sentences means that the examples are not correct English. (An asterisk is used this way in all linguistics books and papers.)

Translated into English, the Hebrew sentences would look like this:

> *The man **that I saw him** was your brother.
> *I read the book **that you read it**.

Most languages form relative clauses in one of these two ways, although in theory there must be many different ways of relating extra information.

Another example of language similarity is that every known language distinguishes interrogatives (questions) from declaratives (statements). Another is that most languages use one of three ways to form yes-no questions. English uses all three:

1 Same form as the declarative but change the intonation:
   You want to go on Wednesday?

2 Invert the subject and the verb:
   Do you want to go on Wednesday?

3 Add a word or phrase to the declarative form:
   You want to go on Wednesday, don't you?

These examples of language similarity do not prove the existence of LAD, but the more similar the structure of different languages, the more likely it is that LAD, or some sort of rule-mechanism that is the same in all of us, has created each different language. In other words, as a linguist would put it, similarity across languages is a necessary, though not sufficient, proof of LAD.

Another argument for the existence of LAD is the speed and ease of child language acquisition until adolescence. This optimum time for language learning is known as the **critical period** and nobody has yet accounted for the

KEYWORD

The critical period: The idea of a critical period is associated with the American psycholinguist Eric Lenneberg (1921–1975), as well as Chomsky. Lenneberg argued that there was a period in their life when animals were better able to learn the behaviour necessary for their survival, and that this also applied to the language learning capacity of humans. This was thought to be because the development of the capacity to learn a language depended on the development of the brain, in particular the development of the language area on the left side of the brain. The process began at the age of two and ended at puberty when the brain was fully developed. The evidence for a critical period remains controversial, as does Chomsky's extension from it that language learning is modularized – that is separate from and independent of other forms of learning.

fact that language learning (usually second language learning) is much more difficult after the critical period has passed.

LAD and the critical period hypotheses would account for the fact that children are often observed to acquire a second language better by exposure to it, rather than being taught it formally. The explanation is that children are born with a series of principles they can use in grammar construction, so that on the basis of a fairly small number of utterances (spoken sentences which children hear) they can construct a working model of the language. This can be done with more than one language during the critical period only.

IS A CHILD FORMING RULES OR RESPONDING TO FREQUENTLY HEARD DATA?

Studying the errors that all children make at certain regular stages, provides further evidence for the existence of LAD, because it suggests that all children are applying rules in the same way, imperfectly at first. For example, all children produce double negative sentences like '*He doesn't know nothing,' at the same stage of their development because the LAD works through the easier double negative to the more difficult single negative – 'He doesn't know anything.'

These errors are not only to do with syntax but also with phonology (the system of sounds). Two-year-old children learning English pronounce 'duck' as 'guck' for a while – all of them do it. And there are other words whose mispronunciation is completely predictable at certain stages of development, for example 'drink' is pronounced 'gik'.

The errors children will *not* make are also predictable. A two-year-old learning English starts expressing negation by putting 'no' or 'not' before one or two word utterances, for example 'no sit here.' Some children put the 'no' at the end – 'sit there no'. But we can predict that children will never put the 'no' in the middle. So you never hear 'sit no there.'

The more predictable the error, or the lack of an error, the stronger the evidence for a rule-based mental process happening. The point is not the errors children make in themselves, but whether or not a rule is deducible from them.

The most ingenious experiment to prove rule-based behaviour dates from 1958 and is still regularly quoted, because it really does establish rule-based language production. The devisor of the experiment was Jean Berko-Gleason who, like Lenneberg as well as Chomsky, Pinker and Skinner, was part of what Pinker describes 'as the Harvard-MIT community' in Cambridge Massachusetts.

What Berko-Gleason did was to ask four to seven-year old children to use a number of nonsense words to see if they could apply language rules to words they could not possibly have heard before, and therefore could not possibly be imitating.

As Elizabeth Ingram explains:

> The words were given meaning and their status as nouns or verbs was established by presenting the children with drawings of animals (or birds or flowers) or of people engaged in various activities. For example the plural of nouns were elicited by showing a card with one animal, then a card with two of them and saying : 'This is a **tass**. Now there is another one. There are two of them. There are two ...'
>
> (*Papers in Applied Linguistics*, OUP, p.238)

Even more famous than the *tass* was the *wug*. The experiment has been known as The Wug Test ever since. The children were shown a drawing with one imaginary animal and then a drawing with two of the same imaginary animals, with the words 'This is a wug. Now there is another one. There are two ...'.

As Pinker points out: 'The children could have refused to answer on the grounds that they had never heard of a **wug** and had never been (taught) to talk about more than one of them.' (*Words and Rules*, 2000, p.14). But that did not happen. Berko-Gleason later wrote that 'Answers were willingly and often instantly given.' No fewer than three-quarters of the pre-school children and ninety-nine per cent of those at school wrote in the correct answer – *wugs*.

The mental process the children must have gone through is the following: A *wug* belongs to the class of things. Things are grammatically expressed by nouns. When there is more than one thing we use a noun plural and most of the time (though not all of the time) that noun plural is 's'. So assuming that this is not a minority irregular case – like the plural of 'child' being 'children' for example – the plural of *wug* must be *wug* + *s* which is *wugs*.

However, if the thought process described in the last paragraph were reasoned out in real time for just one plural, we would not live long enough to produce very many sentences. Clearly the mentalist rules are stored in the mind in a form other than words. How? Chomsky set out to find a system that could possibly account for how, and we trace his journey in Chapters 4 and 5.

But before we leave nonsense words, we can bring experiments with them a little more up to date. Chomskyists like Steven Pinker have found that children treat short nonsense verbs like *pilk* differently from long ones like *ogulate*. In doing so they are (innately, Pinker and Chomsky would say) making a distinction between short Anglo-Saxon based verbs like 'give' and longer Latin based verbs like 'donate.' They (innately) follow syntactic rules based on the difference, for example that you can 'Throw John the ball' but you cannot 'Propel him the ball'. These are mighty claims for children's innate capacity to apply rules to the unstructured input they hear.

And increasingly these claims are being supported by research evidence. Experiments by Hirsch-Pasek at Temple University suggest that infants of four and a half months can tell correct from incorrect sentences (Hirsch-Pasek studied eye movement to indicate the infant's response). Even more startlingly, the infant of four to four and a half months has the same ability in a language other than the one that it will learn. This is strong evidence for some sort of LAD, which later in the child's development is applied only to the language it hears, while rules that would apply to other languages are allowed to lapse or atrophy in some way.

So there is an increasing amount of experimental evidence to support the claims, but they are far from being proved. There is dispute, occasionally even about the interpretation of data. For example, in an experiment at the University of Illinois, the language acquisition of a deaf child was studied. The child's parents were also deaf and they communicated with him in ASL (American Sign Language). The results are disputed. Pinker, following a Chomskyan approach to language acquisition, says that the child had a lower error rate in communication than the parents for certain ASL signs – 20 per cent against 40 per cent. If this is correct, the child must be forming (correct) rules from the parents (incorrect) data, so the child has a rule-forming, LAD-type capacity. How else could he perform better than his parents when his parents are providing the only data he encounters?

However, Philip Lieberman in *Eve Spoke* (Picador, 1998, p.129), taking a basically empiricist line, challenges Pinker's account of the data. We cannot follow the details of the disagreement here, but Lieberman claims that the child 'picks the form that is used most often whether it is "grammatical" or not.'

This makes a huge difference. All such 'frequency' data supports the empiricist position, because it means that what is encountered most frequently (the most powerful stimulus) is imitated and there is no (mentalist) rule-forming at all. Instead, there is what is called 'associative learning'. Many empiricist researchers see a much closer link between animal and human language than Chomsky does – indeed, as we have seen, Chomsky specifically refutes any such link. Who is right? We don't know.

THE EVIDENCE – WILD CHILDREN

There is evidence from another source, which offers clues as to whether the LAD/critical period hypotheses are correct are not. There have been studies made of unfortunate children who have, for various reasons, not been exposed to language at all during the critical period. Because the deprivation that these children suffered was, at least in the early cases, in forests or other places outside towns, they are known in linguistics books as **wild children**.

The case of Genie attracted wide attention for reasons well outside the study of linguistics: 'Girl, 13, Prisoner Since Infancy, Deputies Charge, Parents Jailed' was the headline in the *Los Angeles Times* on 17 November 1970. And Genie had indeed been kept a prisoner in the cellar by her own father and was in a terrible state when she was found at the age of 13 and a half (well within the critical period).

'Her vocabulary comprised only a few words – probably fewer than twenty' Rymer tells us (*Genie*, 1994, p.10). She understood the words for four colours – red, blue, green and brown and the verbs 'walk' and 'go'. Her repertoire of nouns included 'Mother', 'door', 'jewellery box' and 'bunny'. Movingly, in view of what had happened to her, the poor child could say only 'Stopit' and 'Nomore' and, Rymer tells us, 'a couple of shorter negatives.'

KEYWORD

Wild children: The most complete account of wild children is Lucien Malson's *Wolf Children* (1972) and an interesting account of the most significant of them is Rymer's *Genie* (Penguin, 1994). Other than Genie, the most detailed accounts of wild children are Victor, discovered in 1799 aged 11 and later the subject of the film *L'Enfant Sauvage* (1970) by Francois Truffaut, and Kaspar Hauser discovered in 1828, aged 17.

The evidence from wild children seems, on the face of it, to support the critical period theory, in that none of them heard language during the critical period so none of them could speak to any great extent and most could not understand speech. Most attempts to teach speech after the critical period failed but Kaspar Hauser and Genie (who is considered in more detail below) did learn to speak to some extent.

Wild children are still turning up, even if they do not always make it into linguistics books. In October 1999 the BBC showed a programme called *Living Proof* about John Ssabunnya who had been brought up by monkeys in Uganda. The programme discovered that he had invented his own language, which he used to communicate with the monkeys. This completely confirms Chomsky's remark:

'Suppose that a child hears no language at all. There are two possibilities; he can have no language or he can invent a new one.'

(quoted in Rymer, 1994, p.39)

Genie had heard no sounds at all during her imprisonment: no speech, no TV, no radio. When she tried to attract attention by making a noise, she was beaten. She had missed a great deal of development. But after one year of proper care and help, 'Genie's grammar resembled that of a normal eighteen to twenty month old child' (Rymer, 1994). She knew the difference between singular and plural nouns (so passing the Wug Test) and she knew the difference between positive and negative sentences. She was acquiring language. At this point poor Genie's sad life was expected (by others) to prove Chomsky wrong.

However, the result was not quite so clear-cut. Genie's progress stalled. Usually, children's progress with negatives is from '*no have toy,' to '*I not have toy' to 'I do not have a toy'. Genie stayed at the '*no have toy' stage for three years. Also, she could not manage one of the utterances which involves a change from deep structure to surface structure – getting from the proposition, 'the train is coming' to the question 'When is the train coming?'

To sum up, in Rymer's words, 'Genie's hoped for linguistic ascent never materialized.' (ibid, p.128). What do we conclude from that? Not for the first time, we see that you can read the evidence either way.

> ... the syntactic abilities, which both Chomsky and Lenneberg had predicted would be biologically determined had indeed been ... thwarted by her development.
>
> (Rymer, 1994, p.161)

But Genie had also been starved of the frequently repeated input that would, according to the empiricists, promote associative learning. Also, as empiricists like Lieberman were quick to point out:

> One of the major issues concerning Genie's inability to acquire normal competence was whether she was also mentally retarded.
>
> (Lieberman, 1998, p.125)

It could therefore be argued that being mentally retarded, and not a critical period within which rule-forming takes place, would account for Genie's problems with language. Again, we just don't know.

❋ ❋ ❋*SUMMARY* ❋ ❋ ❋

- Chomsky believes that children do not consciously learn language and are not taught it by their parents or anyone else. They acquire it unconsciously.

- According to Chomsky, children are born with a Language Acquistion Device which enables them to apply rules to the language they hear and so produce correct language of their own. The LAD has a physical basis, probably in the neocortex.

- Chomsky and Lenneberg believe that the operation of the LAD is part of a child's developmental process and ceases past a critical period (puberty). Any language learned after that would have to be taught.

- Evidence in support of Chomsky includes the similarity among languages. He is also supported, up to a point, by evidence from experiments and the language performance of wild children.

- Chomsky's empiricist opponents argue that language, which is similar in humans and higher animals, is learned behaviour – acquired and shaped by associative learning following frequent repetition of input.

- Nobody knows who is right but it is possible (tentatively) to say that the weight of the evidence is with Chomsky and his supporters.

4

The Chomskyan Revolution in Linguistics I

Chomsky's views about language have changed and evolved over more than 50 years of linguistic investigation, during which time every word he published and said was scrutinized, analyzed, checked and sometimes criticized. 'Nevertheless the theoretical basis for his linguistic theory has remained constant' and 'Many of the apparent revisions are really clarifications of points which, for one reason or another, had been misunderstood by Chomsky's readers.' (Greene, *Psycholinguistics*, Penguin, p. 24.)

So we will begin at the beginning and look at *Syntactic Structures* (1957) and *Aspects of the Theory of Syntax* (1965) in this chapter, before looking at Chomsky's developments of these fundamental ideas in Chapter 5.

SYNTACTIC STRUCTURES (1957)

In *Syntactic Structures*, Chomsky set out to account for the grammatical knowledge we all have. He was interested in the sound system of the language but he was mainly interested in syntax. He describes syntax as 'the study of the principles and processes by which sentences are constructed in particular languages.' In other words syntax shows you how the words of a sentence fit together – in the popular sense, the 'grammar' of the sentence. In 1957 he was not interested in semantics, the study of the meaning of words, arguing that grammar was autonomous and independent of meaning.

To use a twenty-first century metaphor, syntax is the hard wiring of the sentence. Get that right and your system will work whatever semantic software you put in it.

As we have already seen from the work of Berko-Gleason in Chapter 3, using nonsense words can help clarify how the syntactic system works.

Chomsky did it one year before Berko-Gleason. A nonsense sentence eliminates semantics from the picture, so the study could focus on syntax. Both of the sentences below are nonsense sentences but one of them is grammatical and one is not:

   (1) Colorless green ideas sleep furiously
   (2) Furiously sleep ideas green colorless.

(Syntactic Structures, 1957, p.15)

We all know which of the two is grammatical. It is sentence (1) – incidentally, the most famous sentence in the entire study of linguistics. It is grammatical because we can answer questions like 'How did the ideas sleep?' Answer: 'Furiously.' And 'What colour are the colourless ideas?' 'Green.' The fact that these questions and answers are meaningless makes Chomsky's point for him. Even without meaning we can ask and answer questions based on syntax only. We all understand the hard wiring of language – the grammar. How? Or more precisely, how does the hard wiring work?

Chomsky believes, as we saw in Chapters 2 and 3, that people have a device within them that changes Universal Grammar into the language that the person hears as a child. He devoted a lifetime of linguistic investigation to working out rules that would account for how this change took place. But he did not use the word 'change'. He used the word 'generate'. Chomsky was looking for a **generative grammar** that would account for our ability to understand 'Colourless green ideas sleep furiously.'

KEYWORD

Generative grammar: In this sense, a grammar is a complete set of rules. A generative grammar is a set of rules which can be applied to any words of any language to create sentences that make sense. Chomsky is using the word 'generative' in its mathematical sense. For example, a rule like $x + y = z$ is generative, because if x is 3 and y is 2 it generates an answer – a value for z which is 5. If x is 4 and y is 7 it still generates an answer – 11. In Chomsky's system the z would be a well-formed (that is correct) sentence. He was looking for an $x + y$ type formula that would generate that type of sentence every time.

Chomsky believes that the number of sentences in a language is infinite. Richard Ohlmann's experiment quoted in Chapter 2 supports this very strongly, and arguably actually proves it. Only generative rules, Chomsky argued, can account for (explain) this immense power of language.

But where would a linguist start in the search for these rules? Scientific investigators start at the point where their predecessors stopped. And that was the finite state grammars mentioned in Chapter 2, which looked at a sentence as a string of words going from left to right and tried to account for the next word in terms of what had gone before. For example, you start with a determiner (a word like 'some' or an article like 'a' or 'the') then the next word would be a noun like 'man' then a verb like 'kicked' then another determiner, say 'the', then another noun, for example 'ball.'

    The —-> man ....> kicked ——-> the ——> ball.
    A ——-> woman ....> drove ———-> a ——-> car.

The problem with this is that no language actually works like this. A word cannot always be accounted for in terms of what has gone before. Words often influence other words that are some distance from them in the sentence. For example:

(3) You can have *either* one slice of cake *or* two.
In sentence (3) *either* and *or* are connected but they are not next to each other. Another example:

(4) *John* got up early and washed *himself.*
In sentence (4) *himself,* the last word of the sentence, is dependent on *John,* which is first.

> So any attempt to construct a finite state grammar for English runs into serious difficulties. That is, it is **impossible** not just difficult to construct .... (a finite state grammar) ... which will produce all and only the grammatical sentences of English.
>
> (*Syntactic Structures*, 1957, pp.20, 21)

It is important to keep in mind this restatement of the overall aim: Chomsky was looking for rules that would generate all and only the grammatical sentences of English – the language under investigation – and by extension all languages.

In Chapter 4 of *Syntactic Structures* Chomsky came up with an answer: *phrase structure grammar*. Here, using Chomsky's own example, is how a phrases structure grammar accounts for the sentence:

(5) *The man hit the ball.*
First the sentence is broken into two parts. These are a noun phrase (a group of words controlled by a noun) which is 'The man' and a verb phrase (a group of words controlled by a verb) consisting of 'verb + noun' phrase, which is 'hit + the ball.'

At this point we can note that describing the sentence like this has solved the problem of each word's supposed dependence on the one next to it that we encountered with finite state grammar. But writing the analysis out in a paragraph (which Chomsky did not do) would be too laborious a way to represent the rule. What he did was this:

(i)   Sentence ———> NP + VP
(ii) NP ———> T + N
(iii) VP ———> verb + NP

(Syntactic Structures, 1957, p.26)

The abbreviations are:
  T = the
  NP = noun phrase
  VP = verb phrase
  N = noun + (the + stands for transitive).

Then, after that, the grammatical categories were given a realisation in words. So the analysis continued like this:

(iv) T ——> the
(v)   N ——> man, ball
(vi) verb ——> hit, took etc.

So at this point we have a description of the sentence, which will explain 'The man hit the ball' and 'The man took the ball.' The description consists of the six *phrase structure rules* set out above.

But so far what we have is a static description. How does the brain actually know what to do to get from (i) Sentence ——> NP + VP to (vi) 'The man hit the ball?' The answer is that the sentence is *derived* (Chomsky's term) by applying a series of *rewrite rules* to the phrase structure rules, (i) – (vi) above.

Each of the nine changes listed below can be understood as an instruction to the brain to rewrite, using one of the phrase structure rules (i) – (vi). Here is how the brain gets from 'Sentence' to 'The man hit the ball' in nine rewrites, by applying the six phrase structure rules. The numbers of the six phrase structure rules are shown on the right.

Sentence
NP + VP   (i)
T + N + VP   (ii)
T + N + Verb + NP   (iii)
the + Verb + NP   (iv)
the + man + Verb + NP   (v)
the + man + hit + NP   (vi)
the + man + hit + T + N   (ii)
the + man + hit + the + N   (iv)
the + man + hit + the + ball   (v)

(Syntactic Structures, 1957, p.27)

The six phrase structure rules are sometimes applied out of order, in getting from 'Sentence' to 'The man hit the ball.' John Lyons – Britain's foremost authority on Chomsky's early work – compares this 'with the notion of bracketing in mathematics ...' (*Chomsky*, 1991, p.57) The brackets in x (y + z) tell you that you have to carry out the 'y + z' part of the sum before you multiply by 'x'.

It quickly became a convention to write the rewrite rules not in the way Chomsky did above but in the form of a **tree diagram**.

KEYWORD

Tree diagram: Here is the first tree diagram in *Syntactic Structures*, p.27:

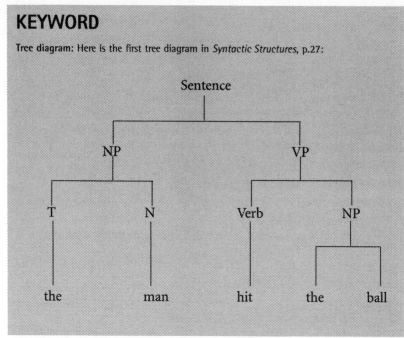

The tree diagram is another way of expressing the list of nine rewrites. In fact, as Chomsky points out in *Syntactic Structures*, it expresses less than the list, because you cannot see from the tree diagram the order the rewrites are to be carried out. But tree diagrams are clear and elegant and have been used in Chomskyan language analysis ever since their early appearance in *Syntactic Structures*.

Phrase structure rules rapidly became more specific, for example on p.111 of *Syntactic Structures* you can find a rule that distinguishes between NP *sing* (that is, a singular noun phrase) and NP *pl* (a plural noun phrase). *Syntactic Structures* also introduced another kind of rule to the phrase structure type rewrite rule: **transformation rules**.

Transformation rules were a way of moving larger bits of language from a sentence to a tree diagram by using fewer rules. They are therefore more powerful than phrase structure rules. These rules, for example, made it possible to derive passive sentences, like 'The criminal

KEYWORD

Transformation rules: A powerful rule that can rewrite more words than a phrase structure rule, accounting for, for example, the difference between active and passive or positive and negative sentences. Instead of having just one element to the left of the arrow, as in phrase structure rules, there could be a 'string' of three or four elements, and the operation carried out by the rule is more complex.

Following Chomsky in *Syntactic Structures*, Lyons gives this example of a transformation – in this case an optional rule when the speaker wishes to say 'The door may have been opened by the man' and not 'The man may have opened the door.' In the string '*Aux*' means auxiliary, i.e. the verb 'to have' or 'to be' used in combination with another (main) verb in combinations like 'may have opened'.

A transformation: 'NP_1 + Aux + V + NP_2 + Aux + be + en + V + by + NP_1' (Lyons, 1991, p.68)

Here is one possible way of representing the transformation as a tree diagram (from Lyons, 1991, p.71)

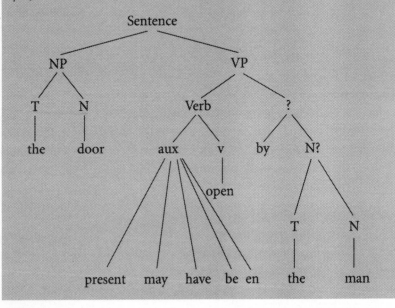

was brought in by the police', from the active form 'The police brought in the criminal.' Negation (forming negatives) and interrogatives using words like 'Does?' and 'Do?' are also derived by transformation rules.

The combination of transformation rules and generative rules has given Chomskyan grammar the name it is most commonly known by – **transformational generative grammar** **(TG)**.

ASPECTS OF THE THEORY OF SYNTAX (1965)

Chomsky never offered any of his linguistic theories as the complete answer to the massive and fundamental issues he was studying. In nearly all his work there is a section where Chomsky himself points out sentences that his theory will not account for. Much of the work on linguistics courses is devoted to these 'problem sentences' and why the system under discussion cannot account for them.

> **KEYWORD**
>
> Transformational generative grammar (TG): Transformational generative grammar (often abbreviated to TG) was Chomsky's system to account for the operation in the brain whereby a Universal Grammar produces rules that generate infinite original sentences from raw language data.

Chapter 5 of *Syntactic Structure* (1957) is headed 'Limitations of Phrase Structure Description'. One limitation Chomsky discusses is conjunction – the joining of parts of a sentence with words like 'and', 'but' and 'so'. A sentence like 'The scene – of the movie and of the play – was in Chicago' (*Syntactic Structures*, p.35) can be derived from the kind of rules that we have seen in this chapter. The problem sentence is one like 'The liner sailed down and the tugboat chugged up the river' *(Syntactic Structures*, p.36) where the two items joined by the conjunction are 'constituents of different kinds' – that is 'sailed down' and 'chugged up'.

Other problem sentences were based on semantic differences. Sentence pairs like:

(7) *John is easy to please.*
(8) *John is eager to please.*

might result in the same tree diagram, because they have the same syntactic structure. However, when the semantics is taken into account, they are very different, because in sentence (7) it is John who is pleased, while in sentence (8) it is other people who are pleased and John who does the pleasing.

In *Aspects of the Theory of Syntax* (1965) Chomsky proposed a syntactic component, a phonological component *and* a semantic component. Meaning (semantics) was therefore brought into grammar; it was something that grammar had to account for. The syntactic component included phrase structure and transformational rules, more united into one system than they had been in 1957.

Another major innovation from *Aspects of the Theory of Syntax* was the notion of deep and surface structure, mentioned in Chapters 1 and 2. In the 1965 version, the phrase structure rules generate a deep structure of sentences. At this deep structure stage, the active and passive would be alike, and so would declarative and interrogative. Transformations then operate, to derive a passive sentence or an interrogative in surface structure. In the 1965 theory, every sentence was held to have both a deep structure and a surface structure.

At that time, many linguists saw the 1965 model, often referred to as the **Standard Theory** of transformational grammar, as a simpler organization of the grammar. The native speaker's knowledge of the difference between sentences like 'John is easy to please' and 'John is eager to please', is to be described in deep structure. That is, the two sentences would have different tree diagrams in deep structure, despite their obvious syntactic similarity. In deep structure, the sentence would be represented as, for example, 'It is easy to please John'.

KEYWORD

The Standard Theory: The 1965 version of TG included a semantic component, including a lexicon to deal with how individual words can combine with other words in the sentence. The standard theory also formally introduced deep structure – it had been implied in *Syntactic Structures* but not stated. Phrase structure and transformational rules were more unified into a single system than they had been in 1957.

'Markers' are signals triggering a transformation. In the 1965 version they also appear in deep structure, triggering interrogatives, imperatives (like 'Shut the door'), negatives, passives and so on. More complex consequences of the difference between these types of sentences and 'simple' active declarative sentences (such as, 'I like fish'), are also found in deep structure.

For example, here is a pair of problem sentences:

(9)   *John weighs the baby.*
(10) *John weighs 80 kgs.*

The sentences are syntactically the same. One aspect of the semantic problem is that we can add 'carefully' to both the active and passive forms of sentence (9), but we can't add 'carefully' – or any other adverb of manner – to sentence (10). In the 1965 version, there is a marker in deep structure saying that an adverb of manner and the preposition 'by' can be added in the passive only, giving us 'The baby was weighed carefully by John'. Sentence (10) cannot be made passive, so we cannot generate the impossible sentence '*John was weighed 80 kgs carefully'.

Another big development in 1965 was the inclusion of a *lexicon*. This was an attempt to specify how individual words can combine with other words. For example we can say 'Sincerity frightens John' and we can say 'John frightens the man' but we cannot say '*John frightens sincerity'. The reason is that 'to frighten' can have an abstract subject, like 'sincerity', but it cannot have an abstract object, because frightening an abstraction does not make sense. In other words, the reason the combination is impossible is semantic.

In *Syntactic Structures*, as we saw earlier in this chapter, individual words (lexical items) could be included in the string of items to be derived. But in *Aspects of the Theory of Syntax* an attempt was made to deal with words by listing them, according to which other words they could combine with. They were put into the second to last string; in other words, they were dealt with late in the derivational process.

For example, let us go back to the now classic '*Colourless green ideas sleep furiously.' This would now be classified as ungrammatical on semantic grounds, because 'sleep' demands an animate subject, 'green' can only be applied to physical objects, and so on. And that would be specified in the lexicon. It would be specified in plus/minus form – a common convention for semantic classification. So 'sleep' would appear in the lexicon as 'sleep + an subj' (animate subject) and so on.

✳ ✳ ✳SUMMARY ✳ ✳ ✳

Syntactic Structures (1957)

• There was some analysis of the sound system, but the main focus was on syntax.

• Chomsky was trying to explain how we got from a Universal Grammar to a limitless number of well-formed sentences. He wanted to find generative rules that could be applied to any language.

• Chomsky used phrase structure grammar to describe the constituents of a sentence – like noun phrase and verb phrase – in terms of each other.

• When the sentence has been described in this way, the brain uses rewrite rules based on the description itself – the phrase structure – to rewrite each bit of the description, until it has been transformed into a correct sentence.

• Transformation rules are particularly powerful rewrite rules.

• For convenience, the rewrite rules are usually set out in a tree diagram.

• The whole system, set out like this, was known as Transformational Generative Grammar (TG).

• A section of *Syntactic Structures* pointed out sentences which TG has trouble explaining. Many of these sentences have semantic differences within the same syntactic structure – for example 'John is easy to please' and 'John is eager to please'.

Aspects of the Theory of Syntax (1965)

• In this book, Chomsky added a semantic component – a lexicon – to the syntactic rules.

• The notion of 'deep structure' was added.

• The 1965 account of language became known as the Standard Theory.

The Chomskyan Revolution in Linguistics II

5

THE LIMITATIONS OF *ASPECTS OF THE THEORY OF SYNTAX*

The introduction of semantic categories in *Aspects of the Theory of Syntax* meant that many more transformational rules had to be devised to stop sentences that are acceptable syntactically, but not semantically (like 'Colourless green ideas sleep furiously'). Here are some problem sentences from *Aspects of the Theory of Syntax*, each requiring a different rule to stop them being generated. The term linguists use for this 'blocking' of deviant sentences is 'constraints'.

(1) * John found sad.
(2) * John elapsed that Bill will come.
(3) * John compelled.
(4) * John became Bill to leave.
(5) * John persuaded great authority to Bill.
(6) *colorless green ideas sleep furiously.
(7) * golf plays John.
(8) * the boy may frighten sincerity.
(9) * misery loves company.
(10) * they perform their leisure with diligence.

(Aspects of the Theory of Syntax, 1965, p.149)

The 1965 Standard Theory needed so many constraints to preserve meaning that the whole system was in danger of collapse.

Suggested solutions fell into two camps. Some followers of Chomsky persevered with developing transformational rules to account for different meanings. This led to an adaptation of the Standard Theory known as the 'Extended Standard Theory' (EST). Other linguists, departing further from Chomsky, tried to reformulate the deep structure rules so that transformations could operate only on syntax. This started another linguistic movement called Generative Semantics.

By the late 1960s and early 1970s, it was becoming clear to Chomsky that the 'phrase structure rules' (like the six rules shown on p.33 in Chapter 4) and what Chomsky called the 'lexicon', which carried the semantic categories introduced in *Aspects of the Theory of Syntax* contained the same sort of information. There was duplication, and in general it was the less specific 'phrase structure rules' that had to be drastically reduced in number.

Here is an example: We are trying to generate sentence (11a) and constrain sentence (11b).

(11a)   John brought the book.
(11b)   *John brought.

The phrase structure rules for (11a) would give us this tree diagram:

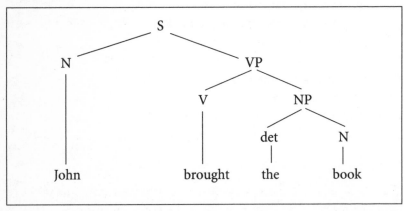

Det stands for determiner. A determiner is anything that can go in front of a noun, including articles, and words such as 'some' and 'any'.

The tree diagram has been derived from these phrase structure rules:

(11a) S ——————> N VP
      VP ——————> V NP
      N ——————> det N

To constrain sentence (11b) however, the lexicon would have to say that 'bring' must be followed by an NP. This is precisely the information provided by the second phrase structure rule in (11a) VP ————> V NP. So, to create a system that will account for the variability of the verb and constrain impossible sentences, like the (10) from *Aspects of the Theory of Syntax* listed above (and there are many more), it is the phrase structure rule that will have to go.

X-BAR THEORY

Rules were needed that were more powerful than phrase structure rules, so that more language could be moved with fewer rules. A rule that could generalize more, by describing language more broadly, would obviously be more powerful in this sense.

Looking again at the phrases themselves, Chomsky realized that, for example, all verb phrases like 'kicked the ball' contain a verb (kicked) plus a noun phrase (the ball). The

> **KEYWORD**
>
> **X-bar:** X-bar theory marked an important change from trying to describe individual rules, to trying to identify the principles which lay behind those rules. That change has lasted until present time.

structure VP ————> V NP occurs again and again, and so it is not necessary to set it out as a rule every time. Similarly, noun phrases and adjective phrases have the same components, so it is not necessary to write those out as a rule every time, either.

If the head of the phrase (the noun, verb or adjective) is called 'X' then what can follow 'X' is predictable and generalizable. A leading British Chomskyan, Neil Smith, gives this example of the generalizability of **X-bar** rules. ('Transitive' describes a verb that needs to be followed by an object, but 'intransitive' needs no object.)

(35) a John <u>mended</u> the car   [Transitive verb]
     b John <u>vanished</u>   [Intransitive verb]
     c John <u>thinks</u> that frogs are mammals.   [Clausal complement verb]

(36) a John is a <u>student</u> of linguistics   [Transitive noun]
     b John is a <u>hero</u>   [Intransitive noun]
     c John regrets the <u>fact</u> that frogs   [Clausal complement
     noun] are amphibians.

(37) a John is <u>fond</u> of Mary.   [Transitive adjective]
     b John is <u>comatose</u>   [Intransitive adjective]
     c John is <u>sure</u> that frogs are   [Clausal complement
     adjective] vertebrates.

(Chomsky: Ideas and Ideals, Smith, 1999, p.67)

PRINCIPLES AND PARAMETERS

Along with the search for **principles** realized by X-bar rules, went the idea of **parameters.** The idea of a parameter is not very different to the idea of a 'constraint'. It is a limitation, something that stops a rule or a process producing unacceptable 'problem' sentences.

For the idea of parameters, Chomsky returned to the learnability problem in child language acquisition. Suppose the Universal Grammar that we are all born with consists not of rules but of principles. The principles operate on the language the child hears, and as the child produces language he or she fixes parameters, which stop wrong sentences.

KEYWORD

Principles and parameters: The idea of principles and parameters was not a system, in the sense that 'TG' was a system. It was a framework within which a system would operate. When the Universal Grammar operated on the language the child heard, it used principles and parameters to come up with a set of either/or choices, which were then applied to the language.

In her accessible account of linguistics, *Teach Yourself Linguistics* (1999) Jean Aitchison gives this analogy of how a parameter works:

… temperature is a parameter of the atmosphere: temperature must always exist, but is set each day at different levels.

(1999, p.208)

Once principles and parameters have operated on language, the child-user is presented with a series of choices, Chomsky suggests, like a series of switches that can be switched one way or the other. The basic options would be innate, inborn, part of the basic apparatus of the brain dedicated to language learning, but the child language-learner would be finding out which option the language they were learning had selected.

Each option would lead to a series of other choices, reverberating throughout the grammar. Some of these choices would be major. It is as if an animal chooses either water or air as the environment they live in – that choice would influence a number of other choices. Viewed that way, the choices can be seen as limited in number but with far-reaching consequences.

Exactly what these choices are in grammar is still being debated. It is really like asking which differences between languages are the most fundamental. One possibility is that there is a choice between having the head (the main word) of a phrase at the beginning or at the end of that phrase.

Aitchison gives the example of the English prepositional phrase 'up the tree', which has the head (the preposition 'up') at the beginning of the phrase. Turkish, literally translated, says 'the tree up' – putting the head at the end. As Aitchison points out, this basic choice has far reaching ramifications for the sentence, as an English sentence like:

> 'The man who fell downstairs broke his leg.' comes out in word-for-word Turkish as:
> The downstairs-fell man his leg broke.

> (Aitchison, 1999, p.210)

Another example is that English keeps to the basic word order of SVO (Subject Verb Object), with very little variation. The fundamental Japanese word order is SOV. All the languages of the world vary these three elements in one way or another. Clearly what Chomsky calls 'parametric variation' (variation by parameter) is a far better way of explaining choices like this than writing out sentence level rules for every consequence of each choice.

The big advantage of the principles and parameters framework, is that it offers a solution to what Chomsky calls 'Plato's problem', which is how children can acquire their first language so easily. Principles and parameters suggests the answer is that language learning is a *selection task* (making choices) rather than an *instruction task* (learning or being taught rules). The learning load is much less with a selection task, because once the correct choice is selected, a whole set of structures based on X-bar theory comes with it.

For example, a child hears the sentence 'Drink this'. The child then works out that it is learning a language like English (or French) which puts the verb at the head of the verb phrase, giving the structure 'V + NP' and not a language like Japanese or Turkish, which would put the verb at the end of the verb phrase, giving the structure 'NP + V' (realized by '*this eat').

Once the child has worked this out, he or she does not have to keep working it out for every new verb phrase they hear. Also, having worked it out, various other structural consequences follow in a *cascade effect*. So one piece of selection-type learning creates a lot of language knowledge.

What we do not yet know is how the child deals with *free variation*. Not all language choices are fixed. Staying in the area of word order, we can say 'I sometimes drink milk' and 'Sometimes I drink milk' and 'I drink milk sometimes' but we cannot say '*I drink sometimes milk'. How does the child language learner know that? We don't know.

Keeping the parameters and principles framework in mind, Chomsky's account of language by the 1980s was this:

* The remaining phrase structure rules (now much more powerful) specified the D-structure (formerly deep structure).

* D-structure became S-structure (formerly surface structure) by transformational operations, which were far fewer and more powerful than the earlier versions.

* PF (phonetic form) rules accounted for the S-structure in terms of sound, and

* LF (logical form) rules accounted for the S-structure in terms of meaning (semantics).

In *Teach Yourself Linguistics* (1999, p.211), Jean Aitchison sums up the process with this diagram:

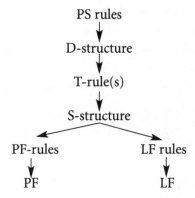

There are differences between all these levels and rules and their predecessors in the 1960s. Perhaps the biggest difference is in the LF rules. Although some of these deal with meaning, others are functional categories, set up to deal with words like 'the' or 'if' or 'wh- question' words like 'what', which do not in themselves carry meaning.

Just to illustrate how far from the standard grammar (of nouns, verbs and so on) linguistic analysis has now come, here is a tree diagram from Smith (1999, p. 84) which shows this kind of analysis applied to the sentence 'What did Harry stir?'

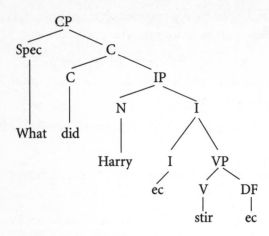

The linguistic rules are becoming more and more abstract: 'CP' stands for Complementizer Phrase, 'spec' is specifier; this and the 'ec' (empty category) show that 'what' has moved from its position after the verb (i.e. 'Harry stirred what?') to a first position, known as a specifier. The 'IP' stands for Inflection Phase to 'reflect the fact that all sentences need some inflection to show finiteness.' (Smith, 1999, p.85).

Smith refers to this as 'a simple example' which illustrates how abstract and inaccessible to the layperson Chomskyan linguistic analysis has become.

I-LANGUAGE AND E-LANGUAGE

At around the time that Chomsky developed the 'Principle and Parameters' idea, he also revised his view of language. As we saw in Chapter 2, the Swiss linguist de Saussure made a distinction between *langue* and *parole*, *langue* being the corpus of a language, *parole* being the knowledge of a language possessed by a speaker of it, a concept that later became known as the speaker's 'competence'. Chomsky, as we saw, wanted to account for competence, but in Chapter 2 of his 1986 book, *Knowledge of Language*, he further refined the *langue/parole* distinction with a distinction of his own.

Chomsky divided all language into I-language and E-language. I-(internal) language is one person's individual language (known in linguistics as that person's 'ideolect'). E- (external) is all other language. The boundaries between I-Language and E-Language could be drawn in a number of places, but it is noteworthy that Chomsky's distinction is another confirmation of his life's interest in the individual, both in linguistics and politics.

GOVERNMENT AND BINDING

Quite often, there are disputes in linguistics about whether the latest direction Chomsky sets is new, or to what extent it follows from what went before. The idea of 'Government and Binding' dates from the early 1980s and in *Some Concepts and Consequences of the Theory of Government and Binding* (1982) Chomsky marked it clearly as a development and not a new direction:

> government-binding (GB) theory ... develops directly and without a radical break from earlier work in transformational generative grammar, in particular from research that falls within the framework of the Extended Standard Theory (EST).

KEYWORD

Government and binding: The idea of 'government' is simply a restatement of the traditional idea that words such as verbs and prepositions can influence the syntax of another word. For example 'I' in 'I love Jane' becomes 'me' in 'Jane loves me', although the same person is referred to, because in the first sentence 'I' is the subject of the verb, but in the second it is the object.

'Binding' looks at the idea of the way in which a word is linked with, or has power over, another word in a sentence. As an example, we can return to a sentence quoted in Chapter 4 (page 32) 'John got up early and washed himself.' The binding in the sentence is between 'John' and 'himself' – two words which are obviously linked but do not follow each other in the sentence.

Chomsky was trying to extend the idea of government beyond the traditional areas of verbs, prepositions, objects and case (categories like accusative and dative, which are found in Latin grammar and influence government in languages like German). The idea of government was extended to refer to any phrase which governed words near it. So in a verb phrase like 'broke the cup' where the old TG tree diagram would be:

```
    VP
   /  \
  V    NP
```

broke   the cup

The idea of government would give us this:

```
    VP
   /  \
  V    NP
```

broke ————————————————>the cup
                governs

'Broke' governs 'the cup' in that it requires 'the cup' (or another noun phrase) to exist. You can see this by putting in a subject, 'John'. Without the noun phrase we get '*John broke.'

Binding comes into the picture more with complex sentences like 'John wrote an essay about himself.' There are two issues here. The first is that the binding occurs between words on different levels of the tree diagram. 'John' is on the second level and 'himself' is on level four (See opposite).

The second issue is the familiar one of constraint, discussed earlier in this chapter. If the idea of government and binding is to account for the sentence 'John wrote an essay about himself' it must also constrain impossible sentences like:

'*Himself wrote an essay about John.'

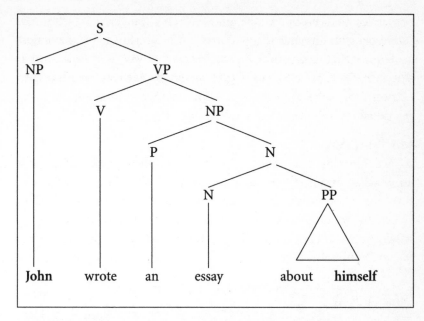

The theory would also have to account for sentences like:

John wrote an essay about Peter hurting himself.
John wrote an essay about Peter hurting him.

In the first sentence it is Peter who is hurt and in the second sentence it is John.

Chomsky therefore set out to be as specific as possible about which part of the tree was influencing which. He and his follows developed the idea of a *c-command*, which stands for 'constituent command', showing which constituents of the tree have power over the others. In terms of the diagram above, the first NP, (John), c-commands the VP (wrote an essay) and all the nodes, or junctions, under it. The main verb 'wrote' c-commands the NP on the same level ('an essay') and every node under it, and so on.

Before leaving this outline of government and binding theory, it is worth noting that these ideas were the first to be developed within the principles and parameters framework. No longer was Chomsky interested only in what was and was not a well-formed (i.e. correct) sentence, as in the days of *Syntactic Structures* (1957) and *Aspects of the Theory of Syntax* (1965). GB (Government and Binding) was trying to account for general principles which underly language and the relationships between words – a huge task.

MINIMALISM

As we have seen, Chomsky himself sees the various ideas and approaches outlined here as a progression, rather than changes of direction. Others disagree. It is certainly true that the core of his ideas remained constant from very early works like *The Morphophonemics of Modern Hebrew* (1949) until his present-day work, which develops the idea of **Minimalism**.

KEYWORD

Minimalism and *The Minimalist Program*: Minimalism is Chomsky's present approach to linguistics. It tries to pare all the rules down to the bare bones, and to find truths that lie behind them. Chomsky is looking for the linguistic equivalent of the basic laws of physics, like gravity, to explain language.

The Minimalist Program (1995) is the attempt to put Minimalism into practice. It involves abolishing the ideas of deep structure (later known as D-structure) and surface structure (S-structure) altogether. In *The Minimalist Program* Chomsky also abandons the attempt to see which level of a tree governs or binds which lower level (see p.51). This is close to abandoning the idea of tree diagrams and phrase structure rules altogether – everything that has been studied and analysed since *Syntactic Structures* in 1957.

As the name implies, Minimalism continued Chomsky's lifelong search for more powerful and simpler rules that would account for (explain) bigger chunks of language data. These rules are contained in a system which 'interfaces between the language faculty and other systems' (Chomsky, in an interview with Domenico Pacitti 'EL Gazette', 9 November, 1999). The 'other', external systems Chomsky refers to, are the ones necessary to produce language, like the vocal chords, the tongue and the brain.

In the interview Chomsky goes on to say that:

> The minimal condition the language condition must meet is what we can call 'the interface condition'. The information it presents must be accessible to the external system. .... Is the language faculty optimally constructed to satisfy that minimal condition? When you pursue this question you're pursuing the minimalist programme.

But the subversive part – the break with the past – came in the realization of Minimalism in *The Minimalist Program* (1995). Chomsky himself put it this way:

> ... the work over the last few years has been ... to try to take point by point the devices that are used in linguistic description and explanation and to show that they're unnecessary, superfluous or incorrect, and that we can get better results by eliminating them.

Smith, in *Chomsky: Ideas and Ideals* (1999, p.86) fascinatingly compares Chomsky to Picasso, in that both constantly subverted their own work, even offending their earlier followers by later revisions of previous ideas. Picasso upset many people who loved and appreciated the paintings of his Blue and Pink periods when he turned to Cubism. On this analogy, *The Minimalism Program* was Chomsky's Cubism, because it appeared to destroy so much of what he had done before.

One of the past ideas that the *Minimalist Program* retained is the idea of 'switch setting', which he had set out in the 'Principles and Parameters' approach. In this model, the lexicon (which basically means all the words) feeds into just two levels of description in the grammar. These are Phonetic Form (PF), representing the pronunciation system, and Logical Form (LF), which represents meaning. When the model first appeared, some linguists talked of 'the end of syntax' – although meaning still has to be regulated by syntax, so we may not have seen the last of it yet.

Here is *The Minimalist Program* (1995) Model:

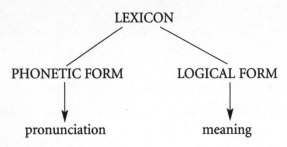

The linguistic principles which guide the system are still being worked out, but a key principle is 'economy', realized by the idea of 'the shortest move'. Here is an example:

a Angela might have come.
b Might Angela have come?
c *Have Angela might come.

The task is to explain why sentence 'b' can be derived from sentence 'a' but sentence 'c' cannot. The principle of economy tells us to look for the simplest explanation. The idea of the shortest move tells us that 'have' in sentence 'a' has got further to travel to get to the 'question position' of first word in the sentence, than 'might' has. That is why English selects sentence 'b' as the correct question form and rejects sentence 'c'.

Chomsky himself regards Minimalism as 'maybe the most interesting thing I've thought of' (quoted in Smith, 1999, p.86), and we now await the insights that will come of it.

* * *SUMMARY* * *

• *Aspects of the Theory of Syntax* (1965) first introduced semantic categories in what became known as the **Standard Theory**, but it was too unwieldy to be workable.

• The first attempt to simplify the Standard Theory was **X-bar theory**, which attempted to develop more powerful rules than the earlier phrase structure rules.

• **Principles and parameters** was a framework of either/or choices, a switch system in the Universal Grammar, which operated on the language a child heard. It was suggested that, in learning language, a child applied principles, rather than learning a system.

• By the 1980s Chomsky analyzed language within a principles and parameters framework in terms of **deep (D) structure and surface (S) structure**. These levels had a complex realization, with terms like Complementizer Phrase, Specifier and Empty Category, which are hardly accessible to the layman.

• In the 1980s Chomsky developed the distinction between I- (**Internal**) **Language** and E-(**External**) **Language**.

• Chomsky's current approach to language is **Minimalism**, which explores the interface between the language faculty and other (external) systems to find universal principles behind language. In applying Minimalism in *The Minimalist Program* (1995) Chomsky has sought to strip away all the various rule systems that he had spent most of his life building up.

6 ... Some Kind of Anarchist

CHOMSKY'S POLITICAL VIEWS DEFINED

Referring to his political views, Chomsky describes himself as 'some kind of anarchist' (*Language and Politics*, p.774).

Later in this chapter we shall look at exactly which kind of **anarchist** Chomsky is, but first let us see where Chomsky's political ideas originally come from.

SOURCES OF CHOMSKY'S POLITICAL IDEAS

Just as he had turned to seventeenth-century France, to Descartes, for his ideas on language and mind, so eighteenth-century France was the source of Chomsky's political ideas – his anarchism. In eighteenth-century France the philosopher **Jean Jacques Rousseau** reformulated the ideas of Descartes into a philosophy of social justice.

The link between Descartes and Rousseau is also a link between the origins of Chomsky's language theory and his political ideas. Chomsky acknowledges this, up to a point:

> The currents of anarchist thought that interest me .... have their roots, I think, in the Enlightenment [the eighteenth-century] ... and even trace back in interesting ways to the

KEYWORDS

Anarchism: Anarchism is a political doctrine opposed to all forms of government. It holds that the highest good is the freedom of individuals to express themselves.

Jean-Jacques Rousseau (1712–1778): In his *Discourse on the Origin of Inequality Among Mankind* (1755) Rousseau argued that mankind should return to a more natural and less corrupt state. But to Rousseau the idea of nature was close to the idea of reason, because human reason was a gift of nature and did not come from the ideas and institutions that man had added to nature. Chomsky wrote that 'the *Discourse* challenges the legitimacy of virtually every social institution, as well as individual control of property and wealth.' (*Language and Freedom*).

scientific revolution of the 17th century, including ... Cartesian rationalism.

(interview with Tom Lane, 23 December 1996)

Elsewhere Chomsky has suggested that Rousseau's ideas could be seen as a development of the Cartesian tradition in an unexplored direction.

Nevertheless, it must again be made clear that Chomsky continues to deny any direct connection between his thought as a linguist and his political ideas.

THE INDIVIDUAL AS A VICTIM OF THE GROUP AND INSTITUTIONS

In his *Discourses* (1755), Rousseau encouraged people to challenge institutions and not be ruled by them – a central belief of anarchism and a deep instinct of Chomsky's:

> I think it only makes sense to seek out structures of authority, hierarchy and domination in every aspect of life, and to challenge them; unless a justification for them can be given, they are illegitimate, and should be dismantled, to increase the scope of human freedom.
>
> (interview with Kevin Doyle for *Red and Black Revolution*, May 1995)

One of the basic 'structures of authority' that should be 'dismantled' is the dominance of parent over child. Rousseau wrote a novel, *Emile* (1762), about the ideal education of a child, concentrating on the child's self-expression rather than its repression from outside. As we saw in Chapter 1, Chomsky was educated in a school which had much the same emphasis.

In the same year that he wrote *Emile*, Rousseau had to flee France because of the anger his ideas were causing. He went first to Prussia and then to England, where he was at first befriended by another man who influenced Chomsky, the Scottish philosopher David Hume.

Chomsky quotes from Hume's *Principles of Government* as follows:

> Force is always on the side of the governed, the governors have nothing to
> support them but opinion. 'Tis therefore on opinion only that government
> is founded; and this maxim extends to the most despotic and most
> military governments, as well as the most free and the most popular.
>
> (quoted in the interview with Kevin Doyle, ibid)

In other words, the group in all its forms, from parents to military
governments, cannot dominate by force. The group has to dominate
with the consent of the individuals it represses. The individual is
tricked, manipulated as Chomsky sees it, into giving this consent. How
people's opinions are manipulated is dealt with in the next chapter. But
here we are looking at Chomsky's and Hume's surprise that people ever
submitted to their rulers.

It is a matter of bewilderment and frustration to Chomsky that people
are duped – as he believes – into obeying authority, hierarchies and
forms of domination. In his interview with James Peck in *The Chomsky
Reader* (1988), Chomsky contrasted the expertise people show when
they discuss sport to the way they discuss international affairs or
domestic problems, at what Chomsky sees as an unbelievably
superficial level.

Elsewhere, Chomsky refers to this duping of the individual by group
hierarchies as 'Orwell's Problem'. George Orwell (1903–1950) was the
author of the classic novel *Nineteen Eighty-Four* (written in 1948,
published in 1949) describing a future society in which history is
rewritten and 'facts' are invented and become true because everyone is
duped into believing them. Chomsky defines Orwell's Problem as 'the
ability of totalitarian systems to instil beliefs that are firmly held and
widely accepted although they are completely without foundation and
often plainly at variance with the world around us.'

Chomsky's world-view, then, is of the individual at the mercy of, and
being manipulated, tricked and duped by, group structures. He wants
the individual to wake up and stop being duped.

CHOMSKY'S FORM OF ANARCHISM – LIBERTARIAN SOCIALISM

Many group structures serve the interests of 'predatory capitalism' which '... seeks only to maximize wealth and power' and is 'antihuman and intolerable in the deepest sense ... and even threatens human survival.' (*Language and Freedom*).

This fierce opposition to the group structures of modern capitalism, drew Chomsky to the form of anarchism of the Russian **Mikhail Bakunin** and the German Rudolf Rocker.

Bakunin rejected the 'purely formal liberty conceded, measured out and regulated by the state in favour of liberty that recognizes no restrictions other than those determined by the laws of our own individual nature' (quoted in *Chomsky's Politics*, 1995, Rai, p.96). So each person's freedom is different, according to their varying personalities and abilities. This is a highly individualistic form of anarchism, which no doubt explains its appeal to Chomsky.

> **KEYWORD**
>
> Mikhail Bakunin (1814–1876): Bakunin led an adventurous life. He was an officer in the Russian Tsar's Imperial Guard, but resigned. He took part in the European revolutions of 1848–9 in Paris and in Germany. He was condemned to death in Austria, but the Austrians sent him back to Russia without carrying out the sentence. He escaped from Siberia in 1852 and ended up in London, where he opposed Karl Marx at the First International and was expelled from the communist party in 1872.

Rudolf Rocker's appeal to Chomsky is at first sight more puzzling. Rocker's anarchism was derived from liberalism and socialism. Many people equate socialism with control by the state, which is why Chomsky's interest in Rocker seems surprising, but the explanation is that neither Rocker nor Chomsky mean state control when they use the word socialism.

As an example of this widespread misunderstanding, George Woodcock, a leading anarchist and author of a classic book on the subject, *Anarchism* (Penguin, 1962) describes Chomsky as a Marxist. Chomsky firmly rejects this description of his political views. He sees

Karl Marx as 'a major intellectual figure' (Rai, 1995, p.95) but dislikes the hero worship attaching to him and to Freud by their followers. Chomsky is not a Marxist, not remotely.

In clear contrast to Marxism, Chomsky's brand of libertarian socialism is:

> a community of free association ... that has achieved its highest forms – though still tragically flawed – in the Israeli kibbutzim; and in the experiments with workers councils in Yugoslavia.
>
> (*Language and Freedom*)

Chomsky also quotes Rocker as saying 'socialism will be free or it will not be at all.' So free individuals come together in communities which get things done without infringing the individual's personality or freedom.

Crucially, the freedom in this community of free associations is guaranteed for Chomsky by rotating participation in administration, so there is no separate class of administrators:

> ... that is, the members of a workers council who are for some period actually functioning to make decisions that other people don't have time to make, should also continue to do their work as part of the workplace or neighborhood community to which they belong.
>
> (quoted in Rai, 1995, p.100)

This is about as far as Chomsky goes on the detail of a better society. There are two reasons for this limitation. The first lies in the nature of anarchism. Once anarchism becomes a doctrine, it ceases to be anarchism because people cannot be free within a doctrine that tells everybody what to do. Chomsky sees anarchism as an approach to life, a tendency of thought and action, which has many different ways of developing and progressing. As soon as anarchism starts to construct blueprints for a new society and allocate roles for it, it infringes its own spirit.

The second reason for the limitation is that it is unfair to expect a critic of a society to offer an alternative worked out in every detail. Chomsky has outlined the sort of society he would like to see – a vision, if you like – and that is all that we have a right to expect. The kind of criticism Rai describes Chomsky hearing from a radio caller – 'Professor Chomsky you are merely a critic of society and you don't have .... a ... political alternative or system that you are clearly advocating' is clearly unfair.

PRACTICAL CONSEQUENCES – THE FAURISSON AFFAIR

Chomsky's actions have always been ruled by his political beliefs. His emphasis on the individual as a creative being and his instinctive opposition to the limiting forces of any kind of organization or group, including those groups he was born into, have had great consequences for his life. He has been accused of being pro-Soviet (and anti-American), pro-Arab (and anti-Israeli) and – ludicrously – he has been accused of being anti-semitic. There has been a lot of what Barsky calls 'mudslinging' (1948, p.178). But never was the mud slung with such force as in the Faurisson Affair.

Robert Faurisson, a professor at the University of Lyon, France, was accused of denying the Holocaust (the murder of 6 million Jews by the Nazis in World War II) and asked to leave his job. He was convicted in a French court for falsification of history.

In 1979, Chomsky was asked by a French friend, Serge Thion, to sign a petition supporting Faurisson's right to express his opinion. Chomsky signed. The French press called the petition 'Chomsky's petition' and Chomsky was accused of holding similar views to Faurisson. Then Chomsky wrote a piece about the civil liberties aspects of the case 'to clarify the distinction between supporting somebody's beliefs [on the one hand] and their right to express them [on the other hand]' (quoted in Barsky, 1948, p.180). This piece was given to Thion, but it ended up being used as the preface to Faurisson's book defending himself.

The identification of Chomsky with Faurisson's views, ridiculous though it was, was damaging enough, but the preface contained one of the very few (possibly the only) examples of carelessness and/or lack of research in the whole of Chomsky's vast writings. Chomsky wrote 'I have nothing to say here about the work of Robert Faurisson or his critics, of which I know very little, or about the topics they address, concerning which I have no special knowledge' (quoted in Barsky, 1948, p.180). The preface also described Faurisson as 'a relatively apolitical liberal of some sort'.

Chomsky's instinctive defence of individual self-expression, the basis of his beliefs both in language and in politics, had got him into this mess but even Barsky, who, with the possible exception of Steven Pinker, is closer to Chomsky personally than any other source quoted in this book, says that the Faurisson Affair 'does tend to throw some of Chomsky's character flaws into relief' (ibid, p.183).

The flaw Barsky mentions is 'his unwillingness to practise simple appeasement when it comes to resolving his differences with those who attack him' (ibid). He might also have mentioned, as many others have done, the occasional excesses of Chomsky's writing style which are so at odds with the gentle personality described by those who have met him.

Here is Chomsky, writing as late as March 1995, so hardly in the heat of the moment, about Faurisson's conviction for falsification of history which 'reeks of Stalinism and fascism and was naturally applauded by the French intellectuals, who proceeded to lie outrageously about it ... the truth being too embarrassing to allow' (Ibid, p.180).

This is 'over the top' and the excesses do Chomsky no favours in argument.

* * *SUMMARY* * *

● The original source of Chomsky's anarchist beliefs is Rousseau, who is linked to the source of his language beliefs, Descartes; so it seems credible that his political and language beliefs are linked, though Chomsky himself consistently denies it.

● Chomsky believes in the supremacy of individual self-expression over any form of group or organization and that individuals are constantly duped into giving up this supremacy.

● The best way to realize individual self-expression in practice is not to have an administrative class; everybody takes turns to share the job of administration while continuing their own work.

● This form of political organization is known as libertarian socialism, an anti-capitalist form of anarchism influenced by Bakunin and Rocker.

● Libertarian socialism is seen in action, imperfectly, in Israeli kibbutzim and workers councils in the former Yugoslavia.

● The details of libertarian socialism are vague, though they are there in outline.

● The practical consequences of Chomsky's political instincts and beliefs have made life difficult for him – especially in the case of the Fourissson affair, where he put an individual's right to freedom of speech above what that individual was actually saying.

7 The Manipulated Society

THE SPECIALIZED CLASS

As we saw in Chapter 6, Chomsky believes that individuals are manipulated and deceived by group hierarchies and he has devoted a lot of his considerable energy to showing how he believes this is done.

Capitalist democracy, argues Chomsky, has developed 'an alternative conception of democracy' which is 'that the public must be barred from managing of their own affairs and the means of information must be kept narrowly and rigidly controlled.'(Media Control Lecture at MIT, 17 March 1991, quoted in *Alternative Press Review,* Fall 1993.)

The people who do this barring of the public from managing their own affairs, Chomsky (following Walter Lippman (1889–1974) editor of the *New York Herald Tribune*) calls the **specialized class**. They are 'the people who analyse, execute, make decisions, and run things in the political, economic, and ideological systems.' (ibid).

> ## KEYWORD
>
> Specialized class: The people who run the country, although Chomsky often implicitly includes anybody working for a large corporation, even in a lowly capacity.

The specialized class are a small percentage of the population. The rest of the people, says Chomsky ironically, 'ought to be sitting alone in front of the TV and having drilled into their heads the message, which says that the only value in life is to have more commodities or live like that rich middle class family you are watching on TV.' (ibid).

NECESSARY ILLUSIONS AND THE MANUFACTURE OF CONSENT

The title of one of Chomsky's books about how people are manipulated into this mindless state in front of the television is *Necessary Illusions: Thought Control in Democratic Societies* (1989).

The phrase **necessary illusions** is a quotation from Reinhold Niebuhr (1892–1971), an American who was a socialist in his early days and then became a leading American protestant theologian. Niebuhr thought that the average person must be given necessary illusions and emotionally potent oversimplifications instead of the truth.

And how is this done? Not by violence. You cannot force people to obey by violence, as the Soviet system once tried to do, Chomsky believes. It is done by propaganda which 'is to democracy what the bludgeon is to a totalitarian state.' (*Media Control*, 1991.)

The phrase the **manufacture of consent** was first used by Walter Lippman in *Public Opinion*, published in 1922. Chomsky and his co-author Edward S. Herman later adapted the phrase as part of the title of their book on the American mass media, *Manufacturing Consent: The Political Economy of the Mass Media* (1988).

In this book, Herman and Chomsky say that:

> the freer the society, the more well-honed and sophisticated its system of thought control and indoctrination will be. The ruling elite, clever, class conscious, ever sure of domination, make sure of that.

One way they make sure of it, one way of manufacturing consent, is by using the tool of the **propaganda model**.

The propaganda model consists of news *filters* that 'narrow the range of news' (*Manufacturing Consent*, 1988). Here is a summary of four of

KEYWORDS

Necessary illusions: Any belief or aspiration which distracts the population from questioning or rebelling against the specialized class.

The manufacture of consent: Controlling the information people receive, so that they all come to believe what the specialized class want them to believe.

The propaganda model: Originally, the propaganda model described five filters which were used to remove news that is unwelcome to the specialized class. The fifth filter was anti-communism, but from the 1990s, Chomsky argues, communism was replaced in the media by other bogeymen, like Saddam Hussein or Muslim fundamentalism.

Herman and Chomsky's filters and how they believe them to work. The summary is from *Manufacturing Consent* unless otherwise indicated.

THE PROPAGANDA MODEL

Filter 1 Size, ownership and profit orientation of the mass media

Media corporations exist to make a profit and ownership of the media is concentrated in a few huge corporate hands. By 1993, 20 corporations owned most of the media outlets in the US. And the process of concentration of ownership is still happening. The AOL-Warner link up is a recent example. (Chomsky interview with Ben Isitt, 22 March 2000)

Even within that concentration there is a 'Media of Influence' – a tiering effect, whereby a few companies have the most prestige, resources and coverage. So 10–24 companies plus the government wire service 'set a framework within which others operate' (*What Makes Mainstream Media Mainstream*, 1997).

They also provide the news itself for most of the lower level media companies. For example, Associated Press sends out a Notice to Editors every mid-afternoon saying what tomorrow's *New York Times* is going to have on its front page. The provincial press does not have to follow this lead, but they do not have the resources not to. And if you are a provincial paper and 'you get off line, if you're producing stories that the big press doesn't like you will hear about it pretty soon. If you try to break the mould, you are not going to last long' (ibid) because the news framework reflects an obvious power structure.

The 24 companies which dominate the media are owned by even larger corporations, usually with assets in excess of $1 billion. Cable TV and the new electronic media have fragmented the market to a degree, but by and large the monopolists have kept control.

'Access to the internet, for example, is through a small number of portals, entry points, and those are by now controlled by major corporations like AOL-Warner' (Chomsky interview with Ben Isitt, March 2000). The corporate structures want the internet 'to focus people's attention on the more superficial things in life, like fashionable consumption, to satisfy what are called invented wants, created wants' (ibid).

Filter 2 The advertising licence to do business

Advertising is the newspaper's main source of income. It distorts the news because it makes the newspaper accountable to its advertisers as well as to its readers. Newspapers that aim for a working class readership are at a disadvantage when it comes to attracting advertisers, because their readers have less to spend. So it is tempting for a newspaper to stop appealing to a working class readership.

Herman and Chomsky turn to England for an example of what happens when a newspaper does not desert its working class readership. When the *Daily Herald* stopped publishing in the 1960s, it had almost double the readership of the *Times*, *Financial Times* and *Guardian* combined. Its readership of 4.7 million people was a loyal one. But it lacked advertising. Some people believe that the Labour Party suffered a decline of influence when the *Daily Herald* stopped publication, because it had no newspaper outlet for its point of view.

Filter 3 Sourcing mass media news

The third filter is reliance on information provided by the government, business and 'experts'. News from sources like the Pentagon and Congress or big business is deemed reliable because of the source. Also, these sources provide a flow of news at low cost. The Pentagon alone, say Herman and Chomsky, has a public information operation that dwarfs any possible dissenting sources. At local level, City Hall and the police department operate in the same way. And as to the experts, most of them are government officials or from conservative 'think-tanks'.

The table on p.25 of *Manufacturing Consent* (1988) shows how many experts on terrorism and defence were government officials, former government officials or members of conservative think-tanks who appeared on one news programme (The McNeil-Lehrer News Hour) in one year. It was over 50 per cent, of all 'expert' appearances, and that excludes foreign government officials.

Filter 4 Flak and the enforcers

The fourth filter is **flak**, used as a means of disciplining the media. Flak is a negative reaction to the news. The overall aim of flak is to criticize the media for insufficient sympathy with US foreign-policy ventures and excessively harsh criticism of US client states.

Flak can be the organization of protesting letters and phone calls, when unwelcome news does get through, or it can be lawsuits or counter-publications. As an example, Herman and Chomsky quote the publication of Peter Braestrup's *Big Story*, which argued that the media's negative portrayal of the Tet offensive helped lose the Vietnam war.

KEYWORDS

Flak: Because control of the media is imperfect, flak is any measure used by the people who own the corporations to bring the news back to what they would like it to be.

Selective perception: Only using news items that suit the specialized class and the corporations.

There are organizations founded to disseminate flak. Two of them, according to Herman and Chomsky, are The Center for Media and Public Affairs, and Accuracy in Media (AIM). AIM, Herman and Chomsky tell us, is funded by large corporations including at least eight oil companies. It puts pressure on the media to follow the corporate agenda and a right-wing foreign policy.

SELECTIVE PERCEPTION

> Public relations is a huge industry. They are spending by now something of the order of a billion dollars a year. All along its commitment is to controlling the public mind.
>
> (*Media Control*, Chomsky, 1991)

One way of doing this is by not telling the people what you do not want them to know. Chomsky calls this **selective perception**. Here is one example of selective perception in the US media, summarized from *Media Control*, (1991).

The Director of the Human Rights Group (CDHES) in the American client country of El Salvador, Hubert Anaya, was arrested and tortured, along with the rest of the group. Ironically, they were imprisoned in La Esperanza Prison, a name which means hope. They were lawyers, and while they were in prison they continued their human rights work. They obtained signed statements from 430 of the 432 prisoners in the prison. The statements described how the prisoners were tortured. One of the torturers was a US army major in uniform.

A 160-page document of their statements, plus a video of the victims testifying, was smuggled out of the prison. But the national press refused to cover it. The TV stations also refused the story. There was one article in the local *Marin County Newspaper* and the *San Francisco Examiner* ran it. Chomsky believes that to be the total coverage throughout the United States. Anaya was later assassinated. The media never asked whether exposure of the atrocities might have saved his life.

Another way of controlling the public mind is the planning and execution of events to fit the needs of prime-time television, says Chomsky in 'Rogue States', a recent article in *Z Magazine*. In April 1986, the US bombing of the Libyan cities of Tripoli and Benghazi was very carefully timed so that it would begin at 7pm Eastern Standard Time, which was when the three major TV channels had their news programmes. And, as Chomsky remarks with heavy irony, 'by sheer accident all three TV channels happened to have their crews in Libya – where of course, they are all the time – so they could film the events as they happened' and then give the administration control of the spin the news was to be given.

THE STUDY OF PAIRED EXAMPLES

In *Manufacturing Consent* (1988), Herman and Chomsky pioneered a technique known as *the study of paired examples*. They chose examples of two closely matching events and precisely measured how the media portrayed them. This pairing technique has been widely praised by Chomsky's followers, but it does present the obvious problem that accurately pairing events from real life is more difficult than pairing, say, examples of language that you have control over.

The class of events studied in *Manufacturing Consent* (1988) was **worthy victims** and **unworthy victims**. An unworthy victim, says Chomsky, is somebody who has been abused by the United States government or its client states. A worthy victim has been abused in an enemy state. Before 1989 and the collapse of the communist world, this would have been a communist country. Today it would be a *rogue state*, that is a country that the United States does not recognize or approve of, like Iraq, Libya or Cuba.

> ## KEYWORDS
>
> **Worthy victims:** Anybody who has suffered at the hands of an enemy of the United States. For example, a Muslim who suffered at the hands of Muslim fundamentalists.
>
> **Unworthy victims:** Anyone who suffered at the hands of the United States or what Chomsky would define as a client state, like a country in Latin America or Israel or even Britain.

Here is an example, from *Manufacturing Consent,* which shows differing media coverage according to whether the victim is worthy or unworthy, using the study of paired examples technique.

Jerzy Popieluszko versus 100 religious victims in Latin America

The worthy victim
A priest, Father Jerzy Popieluszko, was murdered by policemen in Communist Poland in 1984. The policemen were quickly apprehended, tried and jailed. There was an outcry in the United States media and massive coverage of the trial of the policemen. The *New York Times* featured the case on its front page on ten different occasions. Full details of the bloody murder were given and there were allusions to Soviet involvement.

The unworthy victims
One hundred prominent Latin American religious figures were killed in El Salvador, including the Archbishop of El Salvador, Archbishop

Romero. Also four American churchwomen were raped and murdered, allegedly by US-backed security forces. Generally, there was media restraint. Coverage of the Archbishop's murder was big news, but he was an opponent of American actions in El Salvador and coverage reflected that. There was no condemnation of the murder, as in the case of the Polish priest.

Comments in the media included one that a 'basically moderate' government was finding it difficult to control violence of either right or left. Coverage of the trial involving the murdered Americans was muted. In the *New York Times* the hundred martyrs received 604.5 column inches of coverage, just over half the total for Popieluszko.

Talking about the media is not just an academic exercise, warns Chomsky, in the *Manufacturing Consent* film (1982):

> We're not just talking about the media on Mars in the 18th Century. These are real human beings who are suffering and being tortured and starving because of policies we are involved in ... What the media are doing is ensuring that we don't act on our responsibilities.

* * *SUMMARY* * *

- Chomsky believes that America is run by a **specialized class** of professionals and those with power. The rest of the population must be fed with **necessary illusions** to keep them happily watching TV and not questioning anything.

- This is done by the **manufacture of consent**, a propaganda system that ensures that the population believe what the specialized class want them to believe.

- The manufacture of consent is achieved by passing news through **filters** that filter out what the specialized class do not want the population to know. The system of filters is described as the **propaganda model**.

- The media also use **selective perception**, which is simply not covering stories that are not in the interests of the owners of the country.

- Chomsky has reached the above conclusions by studying media coverage using some original techniques like the **study of paired examples** to show media bias.

8 The New World Order

OPPOSITION TO THE VIETNAM WAR

Chomsky has been commenting on and criticizing American foreign policy since the 1960s, when he was an active opponent of American involvement in the **Vietnam War** (1959–75). He wrote an anti-Vietnam war article called 'Call to Resist Illegitimate Authority' in *The New York Review of Books* on 12 October 1966. This led to the founding of an organization called RESIST, which actively opposes American foreign policy.

> ## KEYWORD
>
> The Vietnam War (1959–75): US troops were sent to Vietnam under President John F. Kennedy in December 1961, following an agreement signed with the south Vietnamese. In the war that followed, American troops fought with the south Vietnamese against the communist north Vietnamese, led by Ho Chi Minh. It is estimated that 2 million Vietnamese people were killed in the war and about 3 million injured. There was massive opposition to the war in the USA, especially in the second half of the 1960s, when the fighting intensified. The war ended in April 1975 when American troops pulled out and the north Vietnamese took over south Vietnam.

Chomsky took part in demonstrations and marches against the Vietnam War, notably the demonstration over the weekend of 19–21 October 1967, in Washington, when he was arrested and ended up sharing a cell, briefly, with a fellow protester, the American novelist Norman Mailer. Mailer described the experience in his book about the Vietnam war, *Armies of the Night* (1968). He described Chomsky as 'a slim, sharp-featured man with an ascetic expression and an air of gentle but moral integrity.'

OPPOSITION TO AMERICAN POLICY IN THE MIDDLE EAST

Chomsky has been a critic of Israeli policy toward the Palestinians from the 1960s to the present. He has also criticized what he sees as favourable treatment given to Israel by the American media:

The truth of the matter is that Israel has been granted a unique immunity from criticism in mainstream journalism and scholarship, consistent with its unique role as a beneficiary of other forms of American support.

(*The Fateful Triangle: The United States, Israel and the Palestinians*, p.31)

One example of the favourable treatment Chomsky claims is the lack of coverage of the sinking of the American ship *USS Liberty* by Israeli planes and ships in June 1967, during the Six Day War between Israel and the Palestinians. Thirty-four US sailors were killed and 75 wounded. Chomsky describes the sinking of the ship, which was a defenceless intelligence gathering vessel, as 'clearly premeditated' (ibid, p.32). The Israelis, however, claim that it was mistaken identity. They thought the ship was an Egyptian vessel called the El Quseir.

Chomsky does not offer a possible motive for Israel to deliberately attack an intelligence gathering ship that was helping it in a war; indeed gathering intelligence that would be passed on to Israel. But his view that there was muted media coverage of the event, possibly amounting to a cover-up, seems irrefutable.

OPPOSITION TO AMERICAN POLICY IN CENTRAL AMERICA

Since the 1960s, Chomsky has also opposed American foreign policy in Central America, especially Nicaragua, El Salvador and Panama. In 1985, using the technique of pairing two examples described in Chapter 7, Chomsky gave a talk called 'Intervention in Vietnam and Central America: Parallels and Differences' (Harvard University, 19 March 1985).

Comparing the two interventions he said:

I think we find quite substantial similarities. They are essentially the following:
1 United States intervention was significant and decisive.
2 The effects of intervention were horrifying.

3 The roots of this intervention lie in a fixed geopolitical conception that has remained invariant over a long period and that is deeply rooted in US institutions.

Chomsky defined what he meant by 'a fixed geopolitical conception' in Appendix II of *Necessary Illusions* (1989) when he wrote that 'US planners intended to construct what they called a Grand Area, a global order subordinated to the needs of the US economy and subject to US political control.' In other words Chomsky sees American foreign policy and all its interventions in Central America and in other countries as designed solely to help its own economic interests.

OPPOSITION TO AMERICAN POLICY IN SERBIA

Before 1999 **sovereignty** was not an issue in the various American interventions around the world. But in 1999–2000 there was 'total disdain and contempt for sovereignty' (*Sovereignty and World Order*) when NATO (the North Atlantic Treaty Alliance – in effect the international community's army) first attacked Serbia and then entered its southern part, **Kosovo.**

KEYWORDS

Sovereignty: Sovereignty is a nation's right to rule itself.

Kosovo: The country formerly known as Yugoslavia began to break up into independent regions in 1991. One of these regions was Serbia, whose president was Slobodan Milosevic. Milosevic tried to keep the regions together under Serb domination and used any means to help Serb minorities in the other regions. Kosovo is in south-western Serbia and over 90 per cent of its population is Albanian. It was autonomous (independent, self-governing) from 1946–89. In March 1989, Milosevic ended that independence, putting Kosovo under military occupation.

The international community had first threatened sanctions over the Serb treatment of the Kosovo Albanians. Then, from 24 March 1999, NATO planes, most of them from the USA and Britain, carried out air strikes against Serbian forces and infrastructure (factories, bridges and so on) for 78 days. This was the first time in its history that NATO had ever attacked a sovereign state, breaching its sovereignty.

In response to the bombing, Serbia carried out a plan that they had ready of ethnic cleansing in Kosovo, which meant driving out the majority Albanian population from that region. 'By May 1999 the United Nations High Commission for Refugees (UNHCR) estimated that almost 650,000 civilians had been forced out of Kosovo since March' (*Encarta*). But eventually the air strikes were successful and on 3 June 1999 Serbian President Milosevic accepted a peace plan that allowed NATO soldiers to go into Kosovo and protect the (remaining) Albanians.

Milosevic was arrested on 1 April 2001 for fraud, but with the aim of the international community trying him for war crimes. He was charged with war crimes on 27 May 2001 and his trial at the UN war crimes tribunal began in The Hague in July of the same year.

The President of the Czech Republic, Vaclev Havel said that 'the war in Kosovo was fought "in the name of principles and values" and signalled "the end of the nation state."' (*A New Generation Draws the Line*, Chomsky, 2000, p.1.)

In other words, where the international community thought that a state (Serbia) had ignored the principles and values of the international community, there would be intervention regardless of sovereignty.

Chomsky, in long sections of two books, *Rogue States* (2000) and *A New Generation Draws the Line* (2000) argued bitterly against this. To him the intervention against Serbia in breach of its sovereignty was immoral and wrong.

Chomsky believes that the air strikes should never have been carried out. '... the case for resort to force is weak' (*A New Generation Draws the Line* pp.94–95) and that Milosevic's actions against the Albanians have been exaggerated to the point where they are propaganda, rather than fact: 'Hysterical exaggeration of the enemy's unfathomable evil is a classic feature of propaganda ...' (ibid, p.94).

Chomsky maintains that the only atrocity before the air strikes was the massacre of 45 people at Racak (in Kosovo) on 15 January. All other atrocities, says Chomsky, occurred after the air strikes and would not have happened if the air strikes had not taken place.

Chomsky also follows the author Tim Judah in his book *Kosovo: War and Revenge* (Yale University Press, 2000) in the belief that Kosovo-Albanian fighters, the KLA, 'intended to draw NATO into its fight for independence by provoking Serb atrocities' (US envoy Richard Holbrooke, quoted from Judah in *A New Generation Draws the Line*, 2000, p.105). Chomsky also quotes the British defence minister at the time, George Robertson. He told a House of Commons Select Committee (a committee of Members of Parliament who check government actions) on 24 March 1999 that 'the KLA were responsible for more deaths in Kosovo than the Yugoslav authorities had been' (quoted in ibid, p.106).

As to why NATO should intervene to bomb a sovereign state if it was not to protect the Albanians, Chomsky advances the fact that NATO was celebrating its fiftieth anniversary as an organization at this time and was defending its credibility. He quotes Britain's second most senior defence minister at the time, Lord Gilbert, saying to a Defence Select Committee 'I think certain people in NATO were spoiling for a fight at that time.' (ibid, p.126).

However, Chomsky ignores Milosevic's record in other areas of the former Yugoslavia. Dusko Doder and Louise Branson in *Milosovic: Portrait of A Tyrant* (The Free Press, 1999) say that 'at the end of September 1998, another massacre of Albanians took place at Gornje Obrinje: sixteen people .... were found dead by gunshot wounds at close range.'

Milosevic's record in Bosnia and Croatia has seen him charged with genocide and crimes against humanity in these areas. He has been charged with 'conspiring to wipe out the Bosnian Muslim and Croat ethnic groups in 1992–1995 through massacres, forced deportations, detention and torture' (*Mirror,* 12 December 2001). *The Guardian* (21 January 2002) reports that 'During the Bosnian war thousands of women were tortured and raped by Serbs.' In the face of all this, Chomsky's point that there was only one massacre actually in Kosovo before the air strikes seems marginal, to say the least.

In maintaining that there was no ethnic cleansing before the bombing started, Chomsky, with his usual honest and scrupulous research, quoted evidence from three organizations. One was the State Department's detailed case against Milosevic and his associates in May 1999; the second their formal indictment shortly after by the International Tribunal on War Crimes and the third was the December 1999 OSCE (Organisation for Security and Co-operation in Europe) review (as stated in *A New Generation Draws the Line*, 2000, p.98) But none of these bodies would have had time to investigate, let alone prove, the kind of silent ethnic cleansing that had been going on. In fact, when Milosevic was first arrested the charge had to be fraud because that was all that was immediately provable. It takes time to establish the kind of invisible crimes that took place well enough to prove them in a court of law.

OPPOSITION TO AMERICAN POLICY IN EAST TIMOR

Indonesia had attacked and annexed the island of **East Timor** in 1975 with great violence. The violence was repeated when there were elections on the island for independence from Indonesia in 1999. Chomsky raged with heavy irony at the idea of 'sovereignty' being invoked by the world community to justify its failure to defend East Timor: ' ... Now, it turns out that the sovereignty of Indonesia has to receive delicate and exaggerated respect in this case, even when there is no sovereignty. Because of course Indonesia has no claim to sovereignty in East Timor' (*Sovereignty and World Order*).

What this means is that Indonesia is a client state of the USA and East Timor was under Indonesian control, even though it was taken by

KEYWORD

East Timor: East Timor is an island in the Malay Archipelago, about 420 km north of Australia. It is between the Indian and the Pacific Oceans. It has oil reserves and to the south of it is an important deep-water sea lane which US submarines regularly pass through. East Timor was a Portuguese colony until it was forcibly annexed by Indonesia in 1975. Portugal and Indonesia agreed a referendum on autonomy for Indonesia in August 1999, but elements in the Indonesian government, who were against this arrangement, backed pro-Indonesian militias who carried out atrocities in East Timor, including murder and forcible movement to Indonesian West Timor.

force. Indonesia was seen as having a kind of sovereignty it was not entitled to and 'the US has been directly and crucially involved in supporting the Indonesian invasion, arming it, carrying it through the worst atrocities ...' (Chomsky interview with David Barsamian, 8 September 1999).

Chomsky is surely justified in using the word 'atrocities' for what happened in 1975 and 1999.

Chomsky argues compellingly that the international community did too little too late. Indonesia's economy had collapsed in 1997 and it was dependent on the USA, so the 'limited measures' (*A New Generation Draws the Line*, 2000, p.50) taken did at least force an international presence in East Timor, but not enough was done to help refugees who had fled from the terror. 'The air force that was able to carry out pinpoint destruction of civilian targets in Novi Sad, Belgrade and Pancevo a few months before [i.e. during the air strikes on Serbia – they are all Serbian cities] lacked the capacity to drop food to hundreds of thousands of people facing starvation in the mountains to which they had been driven by the TNI forces armed and trained by the United States and its no less cynical allies.' (ibid, p.51).

Chomsky's main point here is irrefutable and very important, but we can note in passing one of his occasional escalations of language in the heat of the moment. There were no civilian 'targets' of the air strikes in Serbia, as he says. Civilians were killed by the bombing, but NATO planes certainly did not set out to kill them. Chomsky's use of terms like 'war crimes' and 'terror/terrorist' shows a similar escalation of language and sometimes blurs important differences, usually to the detriment of the United States.

But to return to Chomsky's point about the TNI being armed by the United States and its cynical allies; Britain is meant here, and the Foreign Secretary at the time, Robin Cook, does not come out of this very well. As Chomsky points out, as late as 23 September 1999, Hawk Jets, whose delivery Cook had authorised, were arriving in Indonesia to be used against the fleeing refugees.

'According to UN figures the TNI-paramilitary campaign drove an estimated 750,000 of East Timor's 880,000 people from their homes probably some 250,000 to Indonesian West Timor' (ibid, p.51)

However, after Chomsky's books on East Timor went to print, the news from that suffering country got rather better. The United States has continued emergency assistance, as well as reconstruction and development aid to East Timor.

CHOMSKY'S VIEW THAT AMERICA IS A 'ROGUE STATE'

In the 1990s the term **rogue states** was coined for states 'that do not regard themselves as bound by international norms' (Chomsky, *Rogue States*, p.1). But when necessary the United States itself can ignore international law, says Chomsky:

> The US regards itself as exempt ...' (ibid). One example would be when the World Court... condemned the United States for what it called 'the unlawful use of force', in other words war crimes, against Nicaragua, in 1985. The United States refused jurisdiction.

KEYWORD

Rogue state: In conventional politics, the term 'rogue state' is used for an outlaw country that puts itself beyond international norms (international law).

('Sovereignty and World Order' lecture at Kansas State University,
20 September 1999)

That is, the USA refused to accept that the World Court had any authority over it in this matter because it did not like the decision. Chomsky quotes Samuel Huntington in the journal *Foreign Affairs* saying that the US is 'becoming the rogue superpower' (*Rogue States*, 2000, p.47).

But in world politics, America judges some countries as rogue states at some times and not at others, depending – as Chomsky sees it – on whether that country is doing what the US wants at any particular time. For example, Iraq has been a rogue state 'since 1990, when Saddam Hussain disobeyed orders ... But not before 1990 when he was a favored friend and ally, and a recipient of massive aid while he was just gassing Kurds ...' ('Sovereignty and World Order' lecture at Kansas State University, 20 September 1999).

CHOMSKY'S RESPONSE TO 9/11

In September 2001 the world order changed with an event which came to be known by its date 11 September – 9/11 – the day of a terrorist attack on the twin towers of the World Trade Center in New York.

Chomsky's response was: 'To say that Bin Laden is a terrorist, a murderous terrorist is certainly correct, but what about Clinton?' (interview with Evan Soloman, 16 April 2002). In other words United States actions were just as bad as the attack on the World Trade Center.

The mention of Clinton referred to the then American president Bill Clinton authorizing the bombing of the Al Shifa pharmaceuticals factory in Sudan in autumn 1998. It was found to be making medical products, not nerve gas as the Clinton administration had thought, and Sudanese civilians died for lack of these products. Alone among critics of the bombing, Chomsky maintains that it was not a result of mistaken intelligence but 'they knew they were bombing a pharmaceutical factory' (interview with Andrew Billen in *The Times*, 19 August 2002)

Chomsky quickly entered the debate about the response to the 9/11 attack (which he unequivocally condemned). '... it would be hard to find anyone who accepts the doctrine that massive bombing is the appropriate response to terrorist crimes — whether those of Sept. 11, or even worse ones,' *(Terror and Just Response*, July 2002). And '... Attacking Iraq has nothing to do with terrorism. It's establishing our credibility. We must make sure people are scared shitless of us' (Chomsky, in the Billen interview, 19 August 2002).

---

* * *SUMMARY* * *

- Chomsky was an active opponent of US involvement in the Vietnam War in the 1960s.

- Chomsky opposed American foreign policy in Central America. He believes that in this area, in particular, the USA only acts according to the needs of its own economy and to maintain political control.

- Chomsky has been an active opponent of Israel's policy toward the Palestinians and what he sees as favourable treatment of Israel in the US media.

- In Kosovo, the international community ignored sovereignty in the interests of protecting the human rights of the Albanian citizens, wrongly, thinks Chomsky.

- In East Timor, Indonesia was thought by the USA and its allies to have sovereignty, even though Indonesia had seized East Timor. Terrible atrocities were committed there before the international community listened to voices like Chomsky's and stepped in.

- The international community uses the term 'rogue states' for any country which puts itself outside international law. But for Chomsky America is a rogue superpower, which nevertheless decides which states are seen as rogue states by whether they are doing what America tells them.

- The attack on the World Trade Center was wrong, Chomsky believes, but America has carried out comparable if not worse acts and is itself a terrorist state.

Conclusion

Avram Noam Chomsky is one of the intellectual giants of our age, comparable in influence and scope of ideas to Marx, Freud and Darwin – the giants of earlier ages. He stands alone as a great individual and individualist, a natural and instinctive renegade, who cherishes and is fascinated by the life and mind of the individual, and who finds groups, organizations and social forms inimical, impossible, limiting, affronting and offensive.

There is one exception to Chomsky's visceral loathing of groups: the family. He was born into a loving and close family, lived happily within one as a child and he and his wife created one as an adult. Noam Chomsky is a life-long, loving husband and devoted father. If there had been a breath of scandal about his private life, his many enemies would have used it against him by now. He is ultra squeaky clean.

His opponents have met with an equal degree of failure in argument against him. He is formidable, breathtaking, in print and in debate.

Chomsky has expressed his life's work and his essence, his fascination with the individual, in two ways: he has explored how the individual thinks and communicates and he has defended the individual from political oppression, as he sees it, by the state.

In linguistics his main achievement is to transcend linguistics and make the world believe in the individual as a creative entity, not dumb our species down to some sort of reactive machine. He has established the mentalist agenda as the framework within which we explore how we communicate. Other investigators still follow the directions he suggests within that framework. We are, however, no nearer to understanding how human communication works than when he started.

In politics, as Andrew Billen put it in his interview 'For Chomsky, the universal grammar in foreign affairs is ... America invariably behaves disgracefully.' (*The Times*, 19 August 2002.) When America (and the rest of the world) does get it wrong, as in East Timor, he then becomes right and deserves the world's thanks. He is, however, arguably wrong about Kosovo and his reaction to 9/11.

Despite Chomsky's frequent denials that his linguistic and political thought are linked, this book has argued that they are. Even geniuses (and he is unquestionably a genius) have only one brain. The application of linguistic techniques to politics, like the used of paired examples and the taking of small samples of evidence, as he did in his pronouncements on Kosovo, have been far too uncritically accepted by his devoted followers, among whom he has (against his will and to his great embarrassment) been awarded guru status.

He never admits he is wrong, he overuses heavy irony in print, and demonizes anyone who disagrees with him. And he is a moral and intellectual colossus, the like of which the world has rarely seen.

FURTHER READING AND REFERENCE

BIOGRAPHY

Noam Chomsky – A Life of Dissent, Barsky (MIT Press, 1948)
The Chomsky Reader, ed. James Peck (Pantheon, 1988)

LINGUISTICS:

A Short History of Linguistics, Robins (Longman Linguistics Library, 1992)
Chomsky, Lyons (Fontana, 1991)
Genie: A Scientific Tragedy, Rymer (Penguin, 1994)
Modern Linguistics – The Results of Chomsky's Revolution, Smith and Wilson (Penguin, 1990)
Teach Yourself Linguistics, Aitchison (Hodder Headline, 1999)
Words and Rules – The Ingredients of Language, Pinker (Weidenfeld and Nicholson, 2000)

POLITICS

Chomsky's Politics, Rai (Verso, 1995)
Film: 'Manufacturing Consent: Noam Chomsky and the Media Peter', Wintonick and Mark Achbar, Canada, 1982
Bad News Chomsky Archive:
http://monkeyfist.com/ChomskyArchive
Noam Chomsky Resources:
http://www.synaptic.bc.ca/ejournal/Chomsky.ht
The Chomsky Archive:
http://www.zmag.org/Chomsky/index.cfm

LINGUISTICS AND POLITICS

Chomsky. Ideas and Ideals, Smith (CUP, 1999)

WORKS BY CHOMSKY

Politics

American Power and the New Mandarins (Penguin, 1969)
Language and Thought, (Moyer Bell Ltd, 1994)
Manufacturing Consent: The Political Economy of the Mass Media
    (Pantheon, 1988)
Necessary Illusions: Thought Control in Democratic Societies
    (Pluto, 1989)
What Uncle Sam Really Wants (Odonian Press, 1992)
Rogue States: The Rule of Force in World Affairs (Pluto, 2000)
A New Generation Draws the Line: Kosovo, East Timor and the
    Standards of the West (Verso, 2000)

Linguistics

Syntactic Structures (Mouton and Company, 1957)
Aspects of the Theory of Syntax (MIT Press, 1965)
Language and Mind (Harcourt Brace, Javanovitch, 1972)
Lectures on Government and Binding (MIT Press, 1981)
Knowledge of Language: Its Nature Origin and Use (Praeger, 1985)
The Minimalist Program (1995)
New Horizons in the Study of Language (CUP 2000)

INDEX